PRESENTING...
ADRIAN AND CHRISTINE

PRESENTING...
ADRIAN AND CHRISTINE

THE TRUE STORY OF THE
HOTTEST TEAM ON TELEVISION

HENRY LIGHTFOOT

JOHN BLAKE

Published by John Blake Publishing Ltd,
3 Bramber Court, 2 Bramber Road,
London W14 9PB, England

www.johnblakepublishing.co.uk

First published in paperback 2011

ISBN: 978 1 84358 336 3

British Library Cataloguing-in-Publication Data:

A catalogue record for this book is available from the British Library.

Design by www.envydesign.co.uk

Printed in Great Britain by CPI Bookmarque, Croydon, CR0 4TD

1 3 5 7 9 10 8 6 4 2

Papers used by John Blake Publishing are natural, recyclable products
made from wood grown in sustainable forests. The manufacturing processes
conform to the environmental regulations of the country of origin.

CONTENTS

CHAPTER ONE

HOW MANY SHOWS FOR *THE ONE SHOW?*

Older readers will remember when television shut down between six and seven o'clock in the evening. There was only one channel then, the BBC, and the powers that ran it believed that families should be given time to finish their evening meals and get the children to bed, without the temptations, tensions or, for that matter, choices that television broadcasts between those times would surely bring to every household.

The choice was the worrying thing. Best not to trust people with one, because they might pick wrongly and watch the telly instead of reading a bedtime story. They might forget the pan boiling on the stove, ruin the children's supper, and thus tear a hole in the fabric of British society.

In early 1957, ITV had been going for a couple of years in its various different regional guises and was finding the so-called 'toddlers' truce' a giant irritant to its moneymaking ambitions. In those days, ITV was 'a licence to print money', in the words of Roy Thompson, the Canadian 1950s equivalent of Rupert Murdoch, and licensing hours had to be as long as possible. The 'toddler truce', as it was called, would have to go.

As so often happens in broadcasting, it was the BBC who led the way. On Saturday, 16 February 1957, there was a short news bulletin at 6pm, followed at 6.05 by shots of a steam train hurtling along the track to the accompaniment of a song by Don Lang and his Frantic Five. The tune they performed was the title of the new show, *Six Five Special* (over the points, over the points, over the points, over the points), and the contents thereof were mostly music – you know, that new stuff that will soon disappear: rock and roll or whatever it's called – plus some sport and general interest, all introduced by a fresh-faced young groover called Pete Murray and his rather more staid colleague, the lady producer of the show, Jo Douglas.

The general-interest side of things came to the fore on the Monday following, when a new magazine programme began. It went out Monday to Friday, filling in the six-to-seven gap, and it was called *Tonight*. It featured roving reporters such as Fyfe Robertson and Alan Whicker, and a song a night by the gentle West Indian calypso king Cy Grant, or the Scottish folk duo Robin Hall and Jimmy Macgregor. The central figure and anchorman was Cliff Michelmore, an easygoing, friendly, slightly chubby and, for the 1950s, quite informal presenter, although that term 'presenter' had not yet gained currency, nor was it seen as a career discipline.

We often see references to *Nationwide* and Frank Bough as the progenitors of *The One Show*, but Cliff Michelmore and *Tonight* are really more accurately described in that way. Cliff, with his round pudding of a face and his horn-rimmed specs, made his first appearance on *Tonight* more than 10 years before Adrian Chiles was born, and his last with still another two years to go before that momentous event, yet here the seeds were sown. Mr Michelmore might not have been all that happy about going to Birmingham to do his programme, but that was where *The One Show* would come from – at first, anyway.

Adrian Chiles, 'saviour of the BBC's 2006 World Cup coverage' according to one writer, was not a Frank Bough, never would be, nor would want to be, but many people thought that the new programme would be *Nationwide* in disguise. Those who disliked *Nationwide* were expecting (of course) skateboarding ducks and Richard Stilgoe. Others remembered Margaret Thatcher being sunk on the question of the *Belgrano* during the Falklands War by a schoolteacher from Cirencester, and husband Denis complaining that his dear lady wife and Prime Minister had been 'stitched up by bloody BBC poofs and Trots'. They hoped that Adrian would be bringing similar drama to a television time that, on the BBC anyway, was a bit of a quiet eddy in the swirling stream of broadcasting.

Press Release. Category: BBC ONE; Factual & Arts TV

Date: 22.06.2006

Adrian Chiles is to present BBC ONE's new live daily magazine show. The series will run for four weeks this summer at 7.00pm.

Adrian is one of the BBC's most popular up-and-coming presenters. In recent weeks he has received much critical acclaim as the face of the BBC's *World Cup Highlights* programme.

He fronted BBC THREE hit show *The Apprentice: You're Fired* and is the host of the BBC's daily business and consumer programme *Working Lunch*.

The 39-year-old broadcaster also has a loyal radio fan base. He won the industry's top award – a Sony Gold Medal – for his BBC Radio 5 Live (styled Radio Five Live till 2007) show, *Chiles on Saturday*, and he presents the popular 6-0-6 post-match phone-in.

Chris Rybczynski, Editor of the new flagship show, says: 'These shows have provided a platform for Adrian's talents and revealed his ability for talking to the audience in a language they understand and relate to.

'His ability to bridge news, sports and factual entertainment has made him the ideal choice for this BBC ONE flagship programme.'

Mr Rybczynski might also have pointed out that this move would make Chiles the first peak-viewing time presenter, on the prime BBC channel to have a Birmingham accent. The importance of this cannot be underestimated. Birmingham has more miles of canals than Venice and more trees than Paris, but they are all in Birmingham, not in Venice or Paris. Similarly, Adrian's accent may be a mild and non-strident version but it still has its beginnings, middles and endings off the Hagley Road.

Following the BBC's successful *News Hour* between 6.00pm and 7.00pm, the new primetime magazine show will provide a change of pace and tone at the point in the evening when people start to relax and unwind.

Chiles will be supported on-screen by some of the BBC's best up-and-coming talent.

Names revealed so far include popular natural history presenter Kate Humble and undercover journalist Anna Adams who shot to fame fronting the BBC's recent exposé of estate agents.

The series will showcase the work of some of the BBC's brightest new talents, both on and off-screen.

Tessa Finch, Head of Cross Factual Production at the BBC, says: 'The aim is to create a show that will both inform and entertain in the best traditions of the BBC.'

Adrian was seen as the main man, but he needed a main woman too:

Former *EastEnder* Nadia Sawalha will join Adrian Chiles as the co-presenter of BBC ONE's new daily live magazine programme – *The One Show*. *The One Show* is launching later this summer and will feature a lively mix of interviews, factual features and topical stories.

Nadia leapt to fame playing the tough, uncompromising Annie Palmer in the nation's favourite soap. The *One Show* Editor Chris Rybczynski said: 'In real life Nadia could not be more different from the *EastEnders* character that

made her famous. We've chosen her to front
The One Show because of her very warm, bubbly
personality and ability to straddle both hard
emotional issues, current affairs and entertainment.'

We should feel sorry for the lass, what with all that leaping
to fame and straddling hard issues.

Nadia has worked hard to reach the top of her
profession. After training at the Italia Conti
Academy of Theatre Arts, she began in theatre and
took a series of TV roles in shows including
Casualty and *The Bill* before *EastEnders* producers
spotted her star quality and cast her as Annie
Palmer.

Since leaving *EastEnders* Nadia has become a
popular face on BBC1, appearing as a guest on *Test
the Nation* and volunteering to help Comic Relief's
fund-raising effort by signing up for *Celebrity
Driving School*.

Tessa Finch, Head of Cross Factual Production at
the BBC, said: 'Nadia is a great talent. She won
many fans during her time starring in *EastEnders*
where she was an extremely popular member of the
cast. Since leaving, Nadia has continued her highly
successful acting career while developing a new role
as a reporter and presenter. She has a great passion
for live broadcasting and her wide-ranging
experience and brilliant sense of humour makes her
the perfect on-screen partner for Adrian.

'Like Adrian, she is one of the few TV faces who
are equally confident in a factual and entertainment

arena. They are really looking forward to working together.'

Nadia, 41, whose mother is English and father Arabic, comes from a successful thespian family. Both her father and sister – Julia Sawalha who gained fame playing Saffy in *Absolutely Fabulous* – are actors. Nadia says: 'I'm really looking forward to working on this exciting new project with Adrian and the rest of *The One Show* team. I love the excitement of live television – it gives me a real adrenalin rush and I'm a big fan of Adrian's – he's a highly intelligent and very witty man. I think it's going to be lot of fun.'

It would be a lot of fun, but *The One Show* was a risk, as *Tonight* had been and, like *Tonight*, it was an almost instant hit. Admittedly, *Tonight* had had something of an advantage, being the first British television show to be transmitted at that time, and there wasn't exactly a lot else to watch, while *The One Show* was up against the soap *Emmerdale*. In fact, the hope was that *The One Show* would do for BBC1 what *Emmerdale* did for ITV1 – provide a solid platform of viewers from which the rest of the evening could benefit.

And we did say 'almost instant'. Here's one newspaper critic.

Reinventing *Nationwide* was always going to be a tall order. And, if that was the purpose of *The One Show* – new on BBC1 last night – it may just prove too tall. Of course, it's early days and the main presenting duo of Adrian Chiles and Nadia Sawalha did well for a first night and show plenty of promise. Nevertheless, it was hard to discern the programme's core creative purpose.

Well, we can suppose that was one thing it had in common with Tracey Emin's bed. And here are some voluntary Internet comments on the critic's criticism:

I'd like it to be a bit more reactive to events – not necessarily hard news, just the things people are talking about today. And also events that are happening around the UK. I also don't think the programme really suits Nadia Sawalha. Adrian Chiles was brilliant but I didn't think she was so good really.

The One Show has a slight feel of being a bit of a camel – a horse designed by a committee.

The One Show, which started a trial run on BBC1 last night, maintained the proud Brummie track record of mediocrity. It was anything but One. In fact, the several parts never quite came together to make a whole. Adrian Chiles did his usual professional job but he is becoming a bit like presenter Marmite – spread very thinly. You're never sure which Chiles show you are watching. Nadia Sawalha was simply a fish out of water. She looked uncomfortable. 'When I was an actress,' she said – what are you now? – and simply giggles too much.

It is very easy for critics, professional and amateur, to find fault with any TV programme, and more so with a first attempt at a new format. Comparisons with *Nationwide* (many mentions, but no mentions of *Tonight*) may be modified by distance lending enchantment to the view, or the opposite, depending on how many skateboarding ducks you saw, and are only marginally relevant, anyway. However, the general view was that *The One Show* needed a bit of a rocket up its bum, or 'more energy, humour, wit and ambition', if you want to put it another way.

The pilot episodes had featured items on seaside rescue, human sleep patterns and former England cricketer Phil Tufnell, but many critics and other experts felt there was something missing. When Nadia said, 'Wherever you are in the UK, we're going to be telling all sorts of stories about people like you,' pundits thought of *Nationwide*'s rubbish bits.

After one week, *The One Show* had 3.7 million viewers, up 300,000 on its debut. It predictably lost out to ITV1's *Emmerdale*, which had 7.8 million viewers, but easily beat BBC2's *Restoration Village*, with 1.1 million, and *Channel 4 News*, watched by 800,000 people. After the four-week experimental run of *The One Show*, between 14 August and 8 September 2006, it was clear, inside the BBC at any rate, that the risk had been well worth it. Adrian's and Nadia's success inspired many meetings in high places, and plenty of comment in the media, such as:

'*The One Show*, the modern-day successor to *Nationwide* which has played to mixed reviews on BBC1 over the past month, is likely to be re-commissioned without co-presenter Nadia Sawalha.'

Reporters were privy to freely leaked information that BBC executives wanted to give the show a longer run, in expectation of the best bits getting better but acknowledging that the worst bits needed a thorough going-over. That oft-quoted source, the insider, told us that Nadia Sawalha was too inexperienced for a daily live show but did not explain how she might get the experience she needed.

'Adrian is carrying the show,' said a BBC executive. 'The set needs improving,' said another. 'But we get more emails than Radio 4's *Today* programme.'

Even with Nadia thus dismissed as inadequate and the set likewise, the show was attracting upwards of three million viewers on average, almost half an *Emmerdale*, so what could it do when fixed?

Viewers had responded well, but the critics were as vicious as ever. Kevin O'Sullivan wrote in the *Sunday Mirror*:

Relief all round as *The One Show* nears the end of its abysmal experimental run and we can look forward to a future without this patronising pile of TV excrement. Let's hope BBC bosses have worked out what has become only too clear to long-suffering viewers – that hapless hosts Adrian Chiles and Nadia Sawalha are presiding over a nightly calamity that should be consigned to the scrapheap of telly history ASAP.

A former BBC/*Nationwide* man wrote a letter to the papers: 'I've been viewing *The One Show* all this week. Frankly, it's a load of predictable, pedestrian tat.'

A final decision on whether to re-commission the programme, and whether a new co-presenter should be brought in, would not be made for a while but, eventually, to use the BBC's own phrase, the channel committed to 'a nightly pan-UK show', by which was meant a show across the UK, not a show designed to knock everything British.

Nervousness had not been confined to BBC executives. It was a big leap for Chiles, too, coming from business and football and documentaries to a daily show that was meant to generate laughs – and without the ducks. There was also the question of overwork. Although Chiles now quit his last links with Radio 5 Live, handing his Sunday 6-0-6 slot to Spoony, the DJ, there was serious danger of TV overexposure, including, as Adrian was the first to admit, that of his own special take on physiognomy.

An entirely neutral survey of British television presenters and newsreaders would reveal a great preponderance, in the females, of very good-looking ones over those less so, while the men were more evenly spread between the handsome princes and the ugly ducklings. So maybe Adrian's looks wouldn't be too much of a handicap. Look across our TV channels and you will see older and not necessarily lovely men paired with younger and very lovely women: Bruce Forsyth, aged 81, and Tess Daly (38) on *Strictly Come Dancing*; Phillip Schofield (47) and Holly Willoughby (28) on *This Morning* and *Dancing on Ice* (well, all right, some people might find Schofield good-looking); Jeff Stelling (54) and Rachel Riley (24) on *Countdown*.

'No one likes to be called ugly, they just don't,' said

11

Adrian. 'One day my mum is going to get Victor Lewis-Smith.' (Who? See below.) Adrian has been likened to an escapee from the trading floor of a City bank (what do they look like – red braces and hair gel?) and to a barrow boy (as opposed to what – a salesman in Savile Row?). One newspaper reporter wrote that Chiles was 'a gritty Brummie who could pass as [actor] Warren Clarke's son'. We don't know what the two men thought of that, nor do we know what all three parties thought of another witty sally. Robert Key, the Kent and England cricketer, was once said to look like the lovechild of Adrian Chiles and the haggis-faced character actor Jim Broadbent.

Nancy Banks-Smith said Adrian bore 'an endearing resemblance to a very large and embarrassing dog'. Sam Wollaston, of the *Guardian*, wrote of him in the fashion-model episode of *So What Do You Do All Day?*: 'He's like a slightly chubby Labrador who has wandered into Crufts by mistake.' Or, if you were to look in the then current edition of *Men's Health*, you might see before-and-after pictures of Adrian, he having lost four kilos of adipose tissue as part of a project titled 'The Fittest Men in Media'. He had set out to 'visibly change my body shape'. Maybe the four kilos were lost too evenly over his entire physique, because the change wasn't really noticeable.

During the 2006 World Cup, Chiles was described as playing the versatile, utility role, 'the affable, pug-faced Brummie, like Owen Hargreaves with a microphone'.

Adrian once cited an interview he saw with Phil Silvers, a.k.a. Sergeant Bilko, who said that the actor playing Private Doberman – the short, fat, squishy-faced character who was the platoon's fall guy – believed that he was actually Cary Grant or Errol Flynn, brilliantly playing an ugly bloke. Real acting. So that was the way to think about it. Don't be fooled by the ugly duckling. Underneath, there's an elegant swan.

BBC Press Release

Date: 15.11.2006

Peter Fincham, Controller, BBC One, today announced that *The One Show* will return to BBC One next year.

The live nightly show, an engaging mix of interviews, factual features and topical stories from across the UK, made its debut on BBC One last August and proved a hit with BBC One viewers.

When *The One Show* returns presenters Adrian Chiles and Nadia Sawalha will introduce items from around the UK including features from Birmingham and Bristol, current affairs items from Manchester and consumer stories from Cardiff.

Over the course of a year the show will also be going on the road around the UK.

Nations and regions continue to play the central role in *The One Show* and current affairs will also be an essential part of the mix, with reports and investigations every week.

Peter Fincham said: '*The One Show* brings something special and distinctive to the audience throughout the UK – a programme which truly reflects their lives. I'm delighted to make it a regular fixture in the schedule next year.'

Peter Salmon, Chief Creative Officer, BBC Vision Studios, said: 'Long running dramas aside, this is the biggest ever BBC Production commission and is testimony to the skill and dedication of those who worked on the first run of *The One Show*. This is an opportunity to show how the new BBC Vision Studios can link across the UK on massive projects.

Over that first short series of *The One Show*, the final figures showed that 16.3 million viewers tuned into at least one episode and there was an average audience of 3.34 million, representing a 19 per cent share. The peak was 4.1 million, a 21 per cent share.

These figures, plus the faith of BBC1 boss Peter Fincham, were enough. The show was commissioned for another year, with a bigger budget. There were doubters. Even the BBC's chief creative officer, Peter Salmon, thought it would take 'extraordinary measures to pull it off'.

The plan was for *The One Show* to feature content made by BBC and independent production teams from across the UK, which it did; but, as the time approached for the programme to return with a permanent spot in the schedule, 9 July 2007, the inexperienced Nadia was pregnant and had to be replaced, by Myleene Klass. By the end of the new show's second week, it was in the top 30 of the most watched programmes.

Klass soon disappeared, too, to be replaced by Christine Bleakley. This, probably everyone would agree, was when the blue touchpaper was lit, but don't imagine that had been foreseen by the boys from the Beeb. In the

June, they hadn't even realised they had a potential star on the books.

Peter Fincham, BBC1 controller: 'It is great to have *The One Show* back in the schedule – and this time for a whole year. We have a fantastic family of versatile presenters joining Adrian Chiles, and we are harnessing production talent from all over the BBC – from the natural-history unit in Bristol to the current-affairs department through to the consumer unit and entertainment group. The early evening audience is in for a treat.'

One Show editor, Doug Carnegie: 'Adrian is the same bloke on-screen as off it – intelligent and down to earth. He asks the questions viewers want asked, but he essentially likes people. I've even known him be civil to Wolves fans.'

Executive producer Tessa Finch: '*The One Show* is bringing together a great line-up of new and established faces from all across the UK. Our experts all have a genuine passion for their specialist area and our reporters have signed up to travel the length and breadth of the country to find the UK's most fascinating stories.'

Not mentioned by any executive, and listed at the bottom of the press release under 'Other roving reporters', was a certain Christine Bleakley.

Bleakley was living in Belfast, working mostly for the BBC in Northern Ireland and occasionally chipping in with a story for *The One Show*. In London, the producers knew that Myleene Klass had followed Nadia Sawalha into pregnancy, and so were thinking about a successor but hadn't settled on one. Then the matter suddenly became urgent. Without so much as a by-your-leave,

Klass went into labour overnight. By the morning of 5 July 2007, it was realised that a new sofa mate had to be found for Adrian in a few hours.

Bleakley was on her way home from Leeds, having just finished a report for *The One Show*, and was waiting by the carousel at Belfast airport for her suitcase to appear.

'It was ten past eleven,' she remembered. 'Myleene had gone into labour that morning. My phone went, and it was the *One Show* producer. They wanted me in London. Can you come to fill in tonight? Initially I thought no, I can't. I'll just die of nerves. They said my flight was booked at half past one, which meant I had not much more than an hour before check-in and so on. So I said yes, thinking, all right, I'll do it and never be heard of again. Taxi home, bag repacked with clean stuff, back to the airport, and before I knew it I was in the studio. The show went out, it was all over, I'd done the job they asked. At that point I didn't really know if I'd be on again tomorrow, or if Adrian wanted me to be on.'

Christine had arrived that day feeling very nervous and agitated. She didn't know much about Adrian Chiles. She'd obviously heard of *Working Lunch*, 'but I hadn't really watched anything of his. We had the usual ten-minute meeting with everyone. I don't think I made much of an impression on him, and probably vice versa to be honest. I thought Adrian would be a support, somebody to lean on. But he wasn't. I thought he'd be offering to chat through things, but he didn't. He was just focused on the task and expected everyone else to be the same. I thought, I'm never going to do this.'

The One Show presenting team indeed started with

very little between them by way of warming atmosphere. 'It's no secret that I didn't like Adrian to begin with. I found him intense. And I think, as far as he was concerned, I was a nonentity. He acted like a total prat and practically ignored me. But I gave as good as I got and, eventually, that created a chemistry.' It also helped that Bleakley was fully versed in studio workings, more so than Chiles. She knew more than he did about what was possible and what was not. He began to realise that Christine Bleakley was a professional and was not just going to sit there and smile.

'At first,' said Adrian, 'I thought she was a dippy, nice-looking bird, and she thought I was a miserable old fart. But eventually we just clicked. She is technically brilliant. She crosses the *t*'s and dots the *i*'s. What tends to happen is that I put us in trouble, and she gets us out of it.' As they relaxed, they became the best of friends.

Even so, there were doubters. Here's one opinion from a viewer, 'Bewildered of Birmingham', and a few others from those early days with the usual quota of exclamation marks:

I just don't get the whole concept of The One Show. Could someone explain it to me? The whole story about the poor lady whose partner died seemed to miss vital information. For example, why didn't the lady just do what they asked? It seemed like quite a legitimate thing for them to ask. What about other examples? What about companies who do the right thing in these situations? Balance was certainly lacking. Then an (albeit great) actress and comedian was asked her opinion. Apart from

expressing her own personal view (who was
interested in that?) what credentials does she have
to speak on the topic?

And another:

Loved the show tonight (like every night!). Christine
and Adrian, you both make me laugh so much!!

And another:

We try not to miss any of the shows. Thought John
[Jon] Culshaw might have done an impression of
Adrian yesterday. And great to extol the virtues of
BEETROOT.

This, of course, is what Adrian and Christine are all about
– extolling the virtues of beetroot.

Has anyone noticed how like Audrey Hepburn our
Christine looked??... Has anyone else noticed the
resemblance between Adrian and John Sergeant?
They could be father and son.... We just wanted to
let you know that the one thing that makes us
laugh the most is Christine. It is so funny watching
her laugh, she is a real giggler and chuckles at
almost everything! Very entertaining!... I enjoy the
free and easy atmosphere of *The One Show* but I
do wish you wouldn't all talk at once....
Unfortunately, it seems to be commonplace for
guests to be interrupted, or treated to an impatient
'Yeah, yeah, yeah' from Adrian, just as they are

getting into their strides.... Please can you make the autocues LARGER for Adrian and Christine....they always seem to be leaning FORWARD to have to read them!!

As preparation for one evening's edition of *The One Show*, Christine tried to explain to the actor Sir Roger Moore what were the special qualities of a guest appearance on the programme. He seemed to know all about it. 'I know you whiz through things,' he said. 'I think it's a damn good show. My daughter was furious that I wasn't on it months ago.'

It says something for the progress of the show that an octogenarian former Simon Templar (oh, and James Bond of course), who lives in Switzerland, was so up with teatime on the BBC. 'One of the great things about this show is that they can ask you about the other things they've got on the programme that evening,' Sir Roger said.

And he's not alone in being impressed by the conversational feel of the show. Millions of viewers were taking it up the ratings towards the heady heights of the soaps. Adrian said he wouldn't be happy until they'd overtaken *Emmerdale*.

'We're pretty close to ourselves when we're on telly. We've developed an atmosphere where it doesn't really matter if we make a mess of things sometimes.'

Doug Carnegie, editor of *The One Show* as it rose to popularity, said, 'There's something of *The Big Breakfast* about it. Our aim is for a little event that you're eavesdropping on, which means that we move from the plight of Iraqi war veterans to the plight of the natterjack toad. We used to just ask, say, Liam Neeson about his new film; now we require guests, whoever they are, to have an opinion about Iraqi war veterans and natterjack toads.'

But it was not really a chat show as such. The show began with producer Tessa Finch, who defined it as something the BBC has always been especially good at: entertainment with a strong factual element. She thought that: 'At seven in the evening, what the audience wants is something that's informative and educational, but with a spot of glamour too.'

Roughly half the show was live, and half was taped items, some planned many months before. The two presenters arrived at the studio early in the afternoon, to take part in a full and frank dismembering of the previous day's programme, followed by the same on that evening's proposals. With the editor, they worked on the script, with more or less complete independence from executive interference. It was not always so.

'We were struggling for ratings at first, and the channel was twitchy,' said Adrian. 'But it was even worse when the ratings increased because everybody wanted to be a part of the success. Now they've finally relaxed.'

Good word, relaxed. It was the secret of *The One Show*'s success. 'I don't think anyone really expected it to be the success it was,' said Bleakley, 'not because we didn't know what we were doing, but because that's a notoriously difficult slot for television. Traditionally, with a few exceptions, it's been hard to get people to watch at that time. We had the studio, which was important, and we came off the back of the news, and I think at that time of day, that people don't want anything too stressful.'

How stressful is watching Adrian learning how to walk in high heels? With the help of an expert, he elicited this interesting viewer comment:

I went to the workshop last week and I left not only knowing how to sexily and gracefully walk in high heels, I also learned how to walk into any bar and command the room. Needless to say I met a wonderful guy and we had an amazing date last night. I would thoroughly recommend this workshop to all of the *Sex in the City* ladies in London. By the way, I liked Adrian's heels. Could anyone tell me where they were from please?'

More general comments proved the close contact between Adrian, Christine and ordinary folk (if there are such beings):

My husband and I really enjoy the show. You cover some interesting and varied topics. You just know that Christine is going to be giggling her head off on the sofa. I reckon you've got a bit of a man-eater there, Adrian. It has probably all been said before but I think The One Show is entertaining in every way. It is such fun to watch. The far ranging subjects covered in the programme are informative, clear, never dull. The conversation and laughter generated by Adrian, Christine and all the other presenters lifts my spirit.

The show last night, as usual, contained some useful and interesting topics. However, it was spoilt by the rather rude interruption of Twiggy as she was reading out her Five Tips, presumably because of time constraints. The guest list on The One Show is impressive, so why not allow the guests to make a fuller contribution to the show, even if this is at the expense of some of the more tongue-in-cheek items?

Loved the show. Love all the shows. Christine always makes me laugh when she laughs and I thought Twiggy's laugh was just as infectious. Can she take over from Christine when she needs a break from Adrian?

Typical of the show and the developing relationship between the two presenters was the edition on 20 November 2007, when a surprise guest on screen, rather than in the studio, was Christine's sister Nicola. After a brief intro about which sister had the brains and which the looks, Adrian introduced an 'intelligence test', handing Christine a large klaxon with rubber bulb, to squeeze when she knew the answer. Nicola over in Belfast had a pretty little bell to ring.

First question: 'What's the capital of Macedonia?' Christine said, 'She doesn't know that,' while Nicola rang her bell and said, 'Skopje.' That the quiz was fixed became more and more apparent amid the laughter, and the item closed with pictures of the girls when young.

Good, heart-warming, amusing, lightweight stuff. By mid-February 2008, after six months with Bleakley, the show was pulling in 5.7 million viewers. This represented an average audience share of 26 per cent between 7pm and 7.30pm. It had been slowly creeping up in the ratings, hitting 4 million in September 2007 and topping 5 million for the first time in the November.

The One Show narrowed the Monday gap with ITV1's *Emmerdale*, which had lost a little ground to 7.1 million viewers and a 33 per cent share in the same slot, but in the second quarter-hour from 7.15pm, the ratings gap was even closer, with *The One Show* attracting 6.4 million viewers, against 6.7 million for *Emmerdale*. This reversed a trend noticed in the trial run back in 2006, when something like half a million viewers had switched off, or over, around the halfway mark.

'I'd come to London as a temp, a fill-in, not knowing a soul,' said Christine. 'Now I was on a big hit show. Incredible, really, when I'd arrived thinking I'd be soon on the plane back home. So I never take it for granted. I'm an enthusiast, a genuine enthusiast. And I never forget that I was once the tea girl, the one who ran around after everybody, but knowing that the show couldn't happen without people like I was then.'

Could things get even better? Or was *The One Show* really 'a nightly extravaganza of middle-of-the-road televisual slurry', as one newspaper journalist put it? We should have to wait and see.

CHAPTER TWO
THE BOY CHILES

In the year 1800, there was nowhere in Britain, outside London, with a population of 100,000. In the 10 years from 1821, Birmingham, Manchester, Leeds, Liverpool, Bradford and Sheffield all grew by an average of 50 per cent, and by the 1891 census there were 23 places in England and Wales with populations over 100,000. Apart from the capital, Birmingham was by far the largest, home to something approaching half a million folk.

The rest of us lived in smaller towns, or in one of the thousands of little rural communities that were self-sufficient for most of the essentials of life, such as Quinton, Worcestershire. In 1891 Quinton, like so many, was a sleepy village, surrounded by farmland. It was slightly different in that there were a few workshops making nails and suchlike, and a couple of minor attempts at coal mining, but the five miles to Birmingham city centre still seemed a long way by horse and cart, down what we now know as the Hagley Road.

Birmingham, however, was not really so far away at all. In 1910, Quinton became a part of greater Brum, which was in Warwickshire, but on a condition pushed through by the gentlefolk of Edgbaston. The prevailing wind, you see, being southwesterly, blew from Quinton towards the tree-lined avenues and merchants' detached homes of the aforesaid leafy suburb, and so no factories were to be built in Quinton, where their smelly chimneys might discharge unwelcome aromas during tea on the lawn, or disgorge sooty smuts that would inconvenience the laundry maids.

So, in Quinton, the next 60 years saw none of that dirty industry out of which the genteel residents of Edgbaston made their money, but massive housing development caused the almost complete disappearance of greenery. Then came the announcement that a great ditch was to be dug through the middle of it.

The ditch turned into the M5, Junctions 2 to 3, newly opened for business when Mrs Ljerka Chiles, a lady of Croatian birth, produced a son, Adrian, on 21 March 1967. The year had started with the death of Donald Campbell on Coniston Water, as he tried to break the world water-speed record, and it finished with the world's first human heart transplant. In between was the usual mixture of tragedy and comedy, death, destruction, pestilence, war (Israel versus Egypt, for instance), riots, and diplomatic arguments over fish. Britain was applying to join the Common Market, China was exploding her first H-bomb, and Sweden was changing over from driving on the left to driving on the right.

There were also a few bright lights, one or two things that meant something to ordinary people in the UK. For example, colour television started and the Beatles brought out *Sgt. Pepper*. Jimi Hendrix launched his LP *Are You Experienced?*, and over in California it was the summer of love. More seriously for some members of the Chiles family, in particular the baby Adrian's grandfather Arthur, West Bromwich Albion, League Cup holders, lost their second successive final, at Wembley this time, to Third Division Queens Park Rangers, after leading 2–0 at the interval. They finished 13th in the old First Division, which was a decline from the previous year, when the top six had been Liverpool, Leeds United, Burnley, Manchester United, Chelsea and West Brom. Ah, well. Such matters were yet to assert their importance to little Adrian. He had a full six or so years yet to come of relative freedom from Baggies Addiction. (Baggies? See below.)

Father Peter Chiles was a self-employed scaffolder with a growing business and, four years later, the family moved to a more middle-class area, Hagley, a small dormitory town or large-ish village of around 5,000 people, with Birmingham still the main workplace for most of them. (In the 1970–71 season, West Brom finished 17th behind Nottingham Forest and Huddersfield Town.)

The view from Hagley is dominated by the Clent Hills, a modest collection of non-Alpine bumps but very pretty, with woods, architectural follies built by the first Baron Lyttleton, the murder scene of St Kenhelm and other attributes that make the hills a popular destination for tourists. Indeed, a certain well-known presenter of *Match of the Day 2* and other television programmes named the Clent Hills as his favourite hidden tourist attraction.

This can obviously be linked to boyhood adventures –

'Five Go Mad in Clent' – with his friends up in them thar hills, unlike another favourite of his, a doom already mentioned, an affection and affliction that took a hold around the same time and cannot be reasonably explained. With Bromsgrove Rovers and Kidderminster Harriers nearby, Adrian Chiles aged seven, deeply under the influence of his grandfather, instead selected West Bromwich Albion to be his millstone-style neckwear.

Grandfather had similarly influenced his own son, Adrian's father, taking him to all the games as a boy, and the boy had grown into a man who got married and, to get his business into shape, worked on Saturday mornings. Life overtook football. He stopped going, partly, he said, because he hated losing. It made him a misery-guts. Whether being made miserable would ever stop Adrian going, we shall surely see.

The faith mostly involved attending at the Hawthorns, a football ground used by the club since 1900, on the borders with Handsworth and Smethwick. Adrian's first scheduled attendance was for a match against Hull City, which was postponed. He cried all afternoon. Better times lay ahead.

This would be the routine of years. At a quarter past twelve on match days – in those pre-Sky times, all football matches in the four divisions of the Football League started at 3pm on a Saturday – Granddad Arthur would turn up at Adrian's house. Later, younger brother Neville would be picked up too, but in the 1974–75 season only Adrian was old enough to go in the blue Volvo. The ritual surrounding the actual football involved arriving early and leaving early, and took up more time than the match itself.

There would be hardly any cars in the club car park by the time they arrived at around one o'clock. Granddad would go off to the Throstle Club bar for a few pints with his pals, while boy Adrian unwrapped the treasure they had bought on the way, a package of chicken and chips with curry sauce. Even now, says Adrian, 35 years on, if he ever wanted to feel maudlin, to yearn for days of yore, to feel that nostalgic pull of tearful emotions connected with granddad and the Hawthorns and his boyhood, all he would have to do would be to go in a chip shop and ask for chicken and chips and that special, sweet curry sauce they have, that has little to do with proper curry but has a million addicts nevertheless.

The first time this happened was on April 27 1974, a 1–1 draw with Luton Town, who won promotion with that single point. For the next seven years, every other Saturday of the season, young Adrian consumed his chicken-in-the-paper lunch and listened to the car radio on the local station, with all its chatter about West Brom, Birmingham City and Aston Villa, and perhaps the odd mention of Walsall. He never minded being there for so long, getting on for two hours, before Granddad came out of the bar to take him into the ground, nor did he mind their sudden exit ten minutes before the final whistle. Goodness knows how many dramatic equalisers, or winning goals by either side, he missed in those years of ten minute-early departures. It was to avoid the traffic, said his granddad, and Adrian accepted that without question as an adequate reason, and that was why they only *heard* the result, confirming what they'd seen or otherwise, on the radio as they drove home along the M5.

What happened to younger brother Neville, who had been subjected to the same indoctrination, if not for so long? He's a fan, apparently, but not obsessed. He can take it or leave it. The reason he gives for this freedom is that, when younger, and after Granddad stopped taking them, he preferred playing to watching, and so was able to unhook himself from the addiction, to conduct his own exorcism. Or, maybe, he just had the willpower. Like those rare people who give up smoking but can still have an infrequent cigarette without starting the habit again, he can go and watch West Brom now and then, and come away still a free man.

Occasionally there were away matches, to which young Adrian was taken by Granddad in the supporters' coach. One, at Bolton in November 1978, when Adrian was but a lad of 11, had West Brom (or the Baggies) winning 1–0 but, remembers Adrian, they were walking back to the coach after the match when some youths ran past and barged into Granddad, felling him. The boy stood amazed. Granddad was hero, guiding light amid the encircling gloom. Yet there he was on the pavement, just an old man like all the other old men, knocked down by a few ignorant louts. Anyway, he gave a little cough and got up. He took Adrian's hand in his and they went back to the bus as if nothing had happened.

Earlier in that year, in the April, Adrian had been on the supporters' bus with Granddad to Highbury, neutral ground for the FA Cup semifinal against upstarts Ipswich Town, the Tractor Boys, Suffolk bumpkins whom West Brom supporters still thought of as playing in the Third Division South. Ah, but they had Johnny Wark and Brian

Talbot, and they won 3–1, and Adrian cried on the way home. Well, he was only just 11.

Ipswich went on to beat Arsenal 1–0, on a day when Adrian fell off his bike and severely injured his private parts. 'I had to go to hospital to have it all stitched back together,' he recalled. While the Chileses were watching the final on the telly, 'the neighbours kept coming round for a look, so I had to keep standing up and dropping my trousers.'

Even on such a dark day, there was consolation to be had. Ipswich Town had taken the Cup for the first time; West Brom, on the other hand, had won it five times, in 1888, 1892, 1931, 1954 and 1968, and had been losing finalists five more times, and Ipswich had never been losing finalists, so there you are. Old Etonians have won the Cup more often than Ipswich. And more often than Leeds, come to that.

Four years on and it was Highbury again, Cup semifinal again, and their previous nemesis, Queens Park Rangers, but this time it was Terry Venables's team, Second Division (promotion-bound, admittedly), who were in their first ever FA Cup semi. For West Brom, it was their nineteenth semi. How could it be a contest? They had Cyrille Regis.

After the match, Adrian didn't cry on the way home, even though they lost 1–0. He was 15 years old, but on the next seat to him was a large fellow in biker's leathers, at least 10 years older, and he cried until he could cry no more, while Granddad just stared into space, a man who had suffered long and often in the cause and was only doing the same all over again.

At the age of 11, at the start of the 1978–79 season,

Adrian had become a new boy at Haybridge High School, once a grammar school but by then a comprehensive, and quite a big one at that. It was a good school, offering a bright kid like Adrian plenty of chances to shine. Looking back, he claims to have been 'a slightly above-average student'. That it is still a good school can be easily deduced from its internet marketing message:

> Haybridge is committed to delivering a bespoke learning experience for every student which maximises their chances of success throughout their lives. [How many lives can one student have?]
>
> We believe that in order to ensure that students are equipped to succeed in the 21st Century, they must have an education which in addition to securing them the best qualifications possible, builds their confidence and self-esteem by supporting them to develop the skills and competencies necessary to achieve their aspirations . . .

And on another page (questionable punctuation included):

> We aspire to be world class; in both our delivery and outcomes and benchmark ourselves against the best educational practice both nationally and internationally. We work with partners within our Trust and beyond who enable us to offer the most diverse and specialised opportunities.
>
> We look for the most outstanding opportunities for our students to engage with and are tenacious in committing to developmental work which will

enhance the learning experience and ensure that Haybridge remains at the cutting edge of both innovative and collaborative practice.

Haybridge is a school about individuals and it is our vision that everybody feels that they have a voice which can be heard within the school and a personalised experience which enables them to succeed both personally and academically.

Doubtless, Adrian would agree that his education supported him to develop his competencies sufficient unto his aspirations, and in his outcomes he can benchmark himself against the cutting edge of collaborative practice, or something like that, but he probably wouldn't use those words exactly, he being more of a witty straight talker and not one for bullshine.

As we say, he was a clever kid, liked school, liked football – he became captain of the school team eventually – and he had some good fun with the school drama group. One of the plays he appeared in was Mary O'Malley's *Once a Catholic*. Mary O'Malley, née Hickey, from County Cork, was co-founder with her husband Pearse O'Malley of the Lyric Theatre in Belfast. That play of hers is about survival, in particular how children manage to survive a Catholic convent education, as she herself did. Maybe it struck a note with Adrian, who would convert to Catholicism later in life.

Another production he was in was Sandy Wilson's musical *The Boy Friend*. This is a show much favoured by amateur groups, as it has some bouncy tunes, an amusing story and a small cast. Probably the best-known songs are 'I Could be Happy with You' ('If you could be happy with me / I'd be contented to live anywhere. / What would I care / As long as you were there?'), and 'It's Never Too Late to Fall in Love'. The whole atmosphere is of a joyous, lively, hoppity-hop, Charleston mickey-take of the musicals of the 1920s, which must have been right up Adrian's street.

His school nickname was Eggy. He says he doesn't know why. An unbiased commentator might suggest that he should look at the shape of his head and its proportions in relation to his body, and add his reputation for intelligence and quick wit. Anything come to mind?

After school and successful A-levels, and before the fashion for gap years really took off, Adrian spent his year working for his father, before going up to the University of London to read English at Westfield College, originally a women-only establishment but co-ed since 1964. Not one of the major constituents of the university, based in a small set of buildings in Hampstead and soon to merge with Queen Mary College, Westfield promised a student experience quite different from the mass production one might fear at some of the larger institutions. The comedian Bill Bailey went there, three years before Chiles, also to read English, but he gave up after a year.

For the hormone-enriched, dalliance-inclined, young heterosexual male, one advantage of English as a subject, as opposed to, say, mechanical engineering, is that a goodly proportion of fellow students will be female, and even more so at a college with a long history of women only. Adrian had been given to understand by magazine writers and other purveyors of folklore that a lusty lad who can cook *and* make a girl laugh while she's eating his dinners will always be looked on with favour when the inevitable question arises.

His mother, an excellent cook in the Croatian style, offered the thoughtful Adrian a route to girls' hearts that was at once traditional and unusual. If he had his mother's recipes, he could be witty while serving food that was itself a conversation piece. In his own words, he 'thought it might be a seduction weapon'. As it turned out, attractive females studying English and other subjects were happy to eat his food in considerable quantities, and were equally appreciative consumers of his banter and repartee, but the consequences rarely came about as planned.

'I gave those girls magnificent meals, and they laughed their socks off,' he remembered. But that, apparently, was all that came off. 'They said thank you very much and went home.' Still, it gave Adrian a lifelong interest in cooking.

With his degree acquired seemingly without so much trouble and disappointment, despite his description of himself by now as 'definitely a below-average student', he began to cast around for something to do with it. English is the most popular subject to be studied at our universities. Although it equips vast numbers of graduates with a big badge saying, 'I can read the *Guardian* and write whole paragraphs correctly' – no bad thing these days – its vocational implications are narrow. If you don't want to teach it to yet more English students, you are drawn to one of the most overcrowded trades there is: writing. Would-be novelists and poets abound; most of them become teachers, or shelf stackers and hamburger flippers. Journalism, once considered a rather scurrilous kind of occupation, not fit for gentlefolk, has lately become a highly desirable way of making oneself famous, and is therefore also crowded.

In Adrian's day, journalism hadn't quite reached that stage. Long gone were the apprenticeship times, when cub reporters for the local rag stood outside churches in all weathers, anxiously copying down the names of all those attending a funeral: Miss Annette Kurtin, representing Mr and Mrs Justin Flower; Mrs Tracy Lements OBE; Mr Luke Sweet, bearer. And woe betide that reporter if he got anything wrong and someone who was at the funeral was not mentioned and wrote in to complain! Days long gone, indeed, but some of the old-school reporters were still on the staff, and they were waiting for Adrian in Cardiff, had he but known it.

But first there were the two Great Ideas. Number One Idea was the Teaching English as a Foreign Language qualification. Adrian would do the course, then start a Grand Tour of the world in Zagreb, his mother's home town, or maybe Dubrovnik – Croatia, anyway – to get him off to a flying start, as he did speak Serbo-Croat to a certain extent. Perhaps the expected hordes of Croatian lovelies hurrying to his classes would fall romantically for their erudite teacher. Perhaps similar experiences could be repeated in lively capital cities around the globe, where English is seen as the gateway to success. No thought was given to the possibility of dozens of earnest Croatian students, and later those of other nationalities, completing their courses in the belief that the accepted pronunciation of the world's most useful language was that found in Halesowen, Brierley Hill and the nicer parts of Dudley.

Luckily for those Croatians, and for Adrian as it turned out, he went and broke his leg playing football and was forced to retire hurt from the wilder kind of career-oriented pursuits for the moment. He began to think harder about something more homely: his Second Great Idea, the Diplomatic Corps.

Like all would-be civil servants, he had to sit the standard set of exams. The civil service is a calling much favoured by arts and classics graduates on the grounds that, as the objective is to provide information and decisions to the populace across the gamut of their requirements, it's best not to know too much about real life to start with. The exams therefore tend to test potential for high ideals and clarity of mind, rather than the actual hard stuff you might find on a housing estate or in a factory.

Also, you might think it slightly askew that he who would be Her Majesty's naval attaché in St Petersburg, with all its implications of Le Carré duplicity and secrecy, or indeed the British ambassador in Zagreb, should have to sit the same exams as would he who would be concerned with the regulations governing traffic lights or the size and shape of apples, but there you are. Anyway, Adrian failed miserably.

Maybe it was his knowledge of Serbo-Croat that did it but, even as he was already turning his mind towards Plan C, quite unexpectedly he had a letter telling him that there was other government work for which he might be considered. It was signed on behalf of the Director of Establishments, Ministry of Defence, so he ticked the box, posted his reply, and was soon invited for interview at an office in Tottenham Court Road. When he met his interviewer, a rather attractive lady with a certain kind of firmness in her attitude, he was asked if he had his car on a meter, because the interview was going to take three hours.

'Three hours?' said Adrian. 'But I don't even know what the job is.' Always willing to follow a pretty woman, he hobbled along the corridor, dragging a broken leg that would surely have precluded car driving anyway, followed her into an office and sat down to begin the most thorough examination of himself that he could possibly have imagined. Starting with his interests and activities when aged seven, she went up, down and across every little facet of his young life so far, his family's lives, what he ate and drank, which football team he supported . . . After more than two hours, she said she was able to tell him something about the job for which she was interviewing him.

'As you may have guessed,' she said, 'I'm not from the Ministry of Defence. I'm from British Intelligence. I'm from MI5. Here's the Official Secrets Act. Please read it and sign it.' And with that she left the room.

Adrian looked around for hidden cameras, not so much those of the authorities but perhaps ones hired by Jeremy Beadle in an elaborate scam. The lady came back in and allowed Adrian to interrogate her for half an hour, about what the job might involve. He didn't get very far before she called it a day. They, whoever They might be, would let him know.

So, here he was, applying for the job of spy, with the fifth section of the Military Intelligence Directorate. The Cold War was over, so there would be no shenanigans with the Berlin Wall, although there was a great deal of trouble in Northern Ireland and elsewhere – but why could they possibly want him?

'My name is Chiles. Adrian Chiles. A pint of Ansell's, shaken, not stirred.'

No, it just didn't sound right. He hoped that his boasting of Balkan languages had not been too exposed. The memory was still fresh of the time he'd told the owner of a camp site in Croatia that he had only a small rat, rather than a small tent.

For a fortnight he wondered, alternately worrying about why they would be interested in someone who'd failed the exams and, more optimistically, hoping they had spotted some special talent that the exams hadn't revealed. Had he failed the exams in a special way that automatically would be brought to the attention of the spymasters? Was there a psychological test hidden beneath those innocent-seeming questions on history and economics? Did his profile indicate some traits of character that had so far escaped his own and everyone else's attention?

Then the rejection letter came. They didn't want him after all, which he has to admit was the right decision. 'I'd never make a spy,' he says. 'I can't keep my mouth shut.'

He went home to Hagley, leg in plaster, to watch *Match of the Day* and, if there was any on, more football, while his mother fed him as mothers do, in the belief that her son would fade away unless massively and regularly fortified against all eventualities. During his first dinner at home, he regaled his parents with the story of his spy interview. Having popped out to answer the telephone, he came back to find his father creased up with laughter and his mother looking bemused. When Adrian had told them of the lady who said she wasn't from the Ministry of Defence, she was from MI5, his mum had thought he'd said she was from MFI.

Couch-potatodom, boredom, frustration and the inability to say no to another plateful of rasnici and çevapãiçi were all combining to make him feel, you know, not quite depressed but certainly a bit down with life generally. As if he needed any further discouragement, West Brom were about to provide it.

The last game of the 1990–91 season was away to Bristol Rovers, then playing their home games at Bath City's ground, Twerton Park. There were several teams in contention for the second-to-bottom spot, the last place being already and definitely occupied by Hull City. If West Brom won, they would be safe on goal difference, even if Leicester City won as well, and likewise if they both drew. Otherwise, it would be relegation to the third level of English football for the first time in their history.

Adrian was in plaster and so could command a pitch-side position in his wheelchair. The gods seemed to be with the Baggies when the ref sent a Bristol player off a minute or two after the game started, but the result, like six of the previous seven games, was a 1–1 draw. Leicester won their game and so West Brom were down.

Even so, there was life, the universe and everything to think about. His leg would soon be better, he needed something to do, but what? Not for the first time he thought about journalism, and wondered if there were any papers that would take him on. Dear *Birmingham Evening Mail*, I've got a degree in English from London, but I'm a local, and I like football, and I've been sitting on the family sofa for half a year, and I've never tried my hand at so much as a letter to the editor, but will you give me a job? Hmm, probably not.

Father had the idea that some sort of a qualification might help, and there was a well-known school of journalism in Cardiff, so what was stopping him? Of course, in the land of the male-voice choir, laver bread, bara brith and Brain's SA bitter, pursuit of the round football is less of a consideration than the more physical pastime of egg throwing, as the one-eyed soccer fan sees it. Adrian's knowledge of rugby at that point was verging on the nil, but he found himself, by a series of happenstances and serendipitous nods and winks, reporting on a rugby match. It wasn't any old match, either, but one between two of the most followed and most famous clubs, Bridgend and Newport.

His opinion that the rules of rugby were so complex that only the referee understood them, and even he didn't really, was reinforced in the press box that day. 'The ref would blow up for something and I'd ask around me what it was for, and nobody could tell me.' It was only a few hundred words that he had to file, but largely off the top of his head with no time to rewrite and revise. He did it, got his copy in, and worried.

Every aspiring journalist wants to see his or her name at the top of a well-written column, with facts assembled in the right order, linked judiciously here and there with a *bon mot* or a clarifying comment, the whole being a credit to journalism in general and to the bylined tyro in particular. Funnily enough, few think of the other side of the coin. Write a load of inaccurate rubbish and your name's on it.

How accurate Adrian's copy was, we shall never know.

We can safely assume he got the scores and the scorers right. Being Adrian, he may even have managed the odd *bon mot*, but he never had any credit for it because they published it as 'by our own correspondent'.

All that season he covered rugby – amateur rugby remember, before professionalism, which was still four or five years away – and these were dark times for the Welsh. The glory days of Barry John, Gareth Edwards and J. P. R. Williams were gone, and so were a lot of the current stars, to rugby league. The Welsh national team lost all their games in the Five Nations in 1990 and 1991, and were knocked out of the World Cup at the group stage by Western Samoa, prompting that famous remark, 'It's a good job we weren't playing the *whole* of Samoa.'

Still, Adrian had to drive to the grounds, cursing the cost of petrol, which seemed always to be more than the pittances he was earning, to write something about Llanelli and Pontypool. It was good training in some of the essentials of journalism – write coherent sense, write to length, and, if you don't know, don't make it up. Ask. (If only some modern journalists would learn these rules too.)

Even with that experience, plus the training the school had given him, jobs were hard to come by and so he took an opportunity of work experience at the *Birmingham Post*. Maybe he would be sent to cover West Brom's away matches. Maybe there would be expenses-paid trips to Bolton, Sunderland and places like that. If there were any places like that. Instead, the first memory that comes to mind is of an expedition to learn how things were done at the elbow of a sports reporter covering table tennis.

Desmond Douglas, Jamaican born but brought up in

Birmingham and something of a local hero, was playing someone rather less well known to *Post* readers, a Croatian called Zoran Primorac, who himself would go on to great things in ping-pong. To everyone's surprise, Primorac beat Douglas, and Adrian saw his chance. This was a period of turmoil in the home country of Primorac and Adrian's mum. Yugoslavia was collapsing into civil war, as the various components of the former socialist republic tried to assert their independence. The assumption, naturally, was that table-tennis players from such a place would have little English. If *Post* readers were to get the lowdown on Desmond Douglas's conqueror, it would need an interviewer who could speak Serbo-Croat.

In fact, says Adrian, the lad could speak good English but there was no need to spread that information around. Adrian Chiles, interviewer of sports celebrities, was on his way with a story on the back page.

CHAPTER THREE
THE LAD FROM WEST BROM

John Reith, general manager of the British Broadcasting Company in 1922, later managing director of the British Broadcasting Corporation and the 1st Baron Reith, defined the role of the BBC as to 'educate, inform, entertain'. He might have added 'and in that order', because that's how he saw the broadcasting job: a way of educating the masses, with a spoonful of sugar to help the medicine go down. Naturally, in those days, educating anybody required a certain formality. Educators were a class apart. They dressed in academic gowns and spoke with the kind of cut-glass accent with which few feel comfortable now. Translate that to broadcasting in Reithian mode, and you have announcers, always anonymous until World War Two made naming newsreaders necessary (because it was thought the Germans were faking anonymous news broadcasts), delivering their message over the wireless telegraph in those same accents and, after a Reithian edict *ex cathedra* on 4 January 1927, compulsorily wearing evening dress to do so.

Young people today find it hilarious when told that in the 1950s there used to be a ventriloquist, Peter Brough, on the radio with his own show, *Educating Archie*, on the Light Programme (which was to become Radio 2). A ventriloquist? On the radio? Are you kidding? So what would they make of announcers – non-celeb because they were without a name – wearing dinner jackets and bow ties when nobody except the engineers could see them?

Such a culture influenced the BBC for many, many years after the bow ties were taken off. People on the wireless, unless they were 'entertainers' – that is, people of the third rank – had to dress properly and speak properly. Alvar Liddell, voice of the BBC in World War Two, may have worn suit and tie only to work, but there was no doubting the authority in his voice, and in his upper-middle-class Received Pronunciation.

The establishment figures of the BBC in the early 1990s had grown up with the remains of that culture, and so, especially in radio (that is to say the *real* BBC, not those chaps on television and Radio 1 of course), still saw the BBC with a tinge of that light about it.

And then, in 1992, along came a tall, shambolic type of a fellow who had done a bit of sports reporting for provincial papers and who had a Brummie accent. This, according to surveys, is the accent found most unpleasing by most people not from Birmingham. Having such an accent is also more likely (according to surveys) to be a cause of discrimination at work than sex, race, religion, gender, age or anything else covered by the law. Quite what the PC/equality agitators were doing when the law was drafted we don't know. Having a Brum/Geordie/ Lancashire (or, indeed, Northern Irish) accent could be a fertile area for blame/claim lawyers, were there any laws about it. In any case, not many years before, Adrian would have done his work experience and been shown the door. Not so by this time.

'They assumed I was thick because of my accent, so all I had to do to impress them was string a couple of sentences together.' Yes, well, there was a bit more to it than that, Adrian, such as a certain amount of natural ability. In any case, as he readily admits, his accent is West Midlands middle, more Brummie Lite than authentic Longbridge Working Men's Club.

Whatever, the gentle regional intonation fitted perfectly with his own relaxed delivery, and he did well enough in his work experience with the BBC Business Unit to be offered work in the backrooms of radio business programmes. In this fairly quiet environment, not exactly in the glaring spotlight, once he got in and showed he was a valuable team member, he could be tried out as a presenter without too much of a risk to the chandeliers.

'There is only one thing that you need to be a presenter,' Adrian said later, 'and that is to find someone daft enough to give you something to present. The bloke who gave me my first chance was Alan Griffiths, boss of BBC radio business programmes, where I'd gone on an attachment from BBC1's *Business Breakfast*. Why anyone would give me something to present, I don't know. I've got a funny accent and I didn't know my arse from my elbow. But Alan put me on the World Service business news and then he gave me *The Financial World Tonight* on Radio 4 to present a few times, which was a crazy thing to do.'

The biggest influence on Adrian and his career was Paul Gibbs, then editor of *Business Breakfast*, where he had first started on work experience. Gibbs gave Adrian a proper job as a researcher, and then as a producer, although – Adrian says – the new boy was hardly qualified.

'He also sent me on mad assignments. I'd only been there eight months when he sent me to Yugoslavia in the middle of the Balkan War, to do a film on the economic implications. Another time, he gave me an item to produce even though I didn't know the first thing about it. I couldn't get it right, so I went to his house on the Sunday night. He told me it was crap and showed me how to reinvent it.'

That was in 1993. Less than a year later, Adrian had made himself into a regular on Radio 5 Live, just re-launched, giving the business news, 'Wake Up to Money', then part of the breakfast show, which was anchored by Peter Allen and the owner of the first voice to be heard on the new Radio 5 Live, Jane Garvey.

Garvey, almost a Scouser (seeing that she was from Crosby), a football fan (Liverpool, indoctrinated by her father Ray) and a graduate of Birmingham University after Merchant Taylors' Girls School in Liverpool, had a lot in common with her new junior business reporter. She'd come up through the provinces, too, joining BBC Radio Hereford and Worcester on the microphone after starting out in advertising, then moving to editorial jobs at the music station, Radio Wyvern. Radio Hereford and Worcester promoted her to be the anchor of their breakfast show, and from there she stepped up to national BBC with Radio 5 Live. Like her husband-to-be Brummie, she attracted vituperation as well as compliments. If all the insults were added together, she says, she could have been described as a 'rabid, appalling, hairy feminist who dared to talk about football'.

Daring to talk about football was fine by Adrian, but, if it was love at first sight, nobody mentioned it for quite a while. 'We were slow movers,' he says. 'It took us eighteen months or more to get it together.'

Part of the blame for that must rest with Adrian. He'd had a steady relationship that had broken up, so he had this brilliant idea of sending Jane a Valentine's card, anonymously, of course, as you do. Eagerly awaiting her reaction, he was devastated to note her smiling acceptance of the message of love while attributing it not to him but to another fellow. And she started going out with that man, and he hadn't sent the Valentine, although he was happy to take the credit.

Adrian's career was another slow mover, but there were reasons for that, mainly connected with his personality. He has never, he claims, had a game plan. To him, the idea of setting out in determined fashion to be a nationally popular, famous and instantly recognisable television star would have been as realistic as borrowing money on the strength of his future wages as scheming midfield general for West Bromwich Albion. The idea never occurred to him to attempt to climb Everest naked, or to form a rock-and-roll band. He simply thought he liked being a journalist, so he would see where that might take him – if he thought as far ahead as that.

There are people in the world who plan exactly how things will go. They get a postgraduate qualification in accountancy or law, or they join an insurance company, and they know just where they expect to be at retirement age. Or, if they want to be celebs, they pester and pester and nag and nag and make themselves nuisances until someone out of sheer desperation gives them a trial on the graveyard slot on Channel 927. That was not the way of Adrian Chiles. Of course, he's not a shrinking violet exactly. Nobody rises to the top of the fishpond of television without doing a bit of swimming. But he claims never to have begged, never to have telephoned a producer to insist that he, Chiles, was the very man the world needed for whatever vacancy was on the go at the time.

One report Adrian did for Radio 5 Live was on showbiz agents and their business, and this led him to interview Johnny Vaughan. Only one year older than Adrian, Vaughan had come from a decidedly patchy youth, including a longish term in prison after being set up in a drugs deal. 'The police were convinced I was Mr. Big. In fact, I was just a fool,' he told the *Mail*. The experience, he has said, made him re-evaluate his life. He had had a lucky break into television, with Channel 4 and a late-night film-review programme, around the time that Adrian had begun his work experience with BBC radio. The contrast between the two men was considerable. One was a Brummie lad from a working-class background, a foot soldier on business news, broadcast at times when listening audiences could not have been huge. The other was a public-schoolboy TV star now fronting *The Big Breakfast*, who supported Chelsea and had no obvious prior broadcasting qualifications apart from his personality.

Adrian asked Vaughan about the secret of his success, and the answer was a proverb, 'Slow for the dough, play it fast and it won't last', which is attributed to various sporting and celebrity figures but was probably made up on the spot by Vaughan. In any case, it hardly matched Vaughan's own career, although Adrian Chiles could see the sense of it when it was applied to himself. If he could also have seen the future, he would perhaps have been amused by a couple of things. One was getting into a crowded lift at Television Centre a few years later, by which time Vaughan had been paid a six-figure sum to present his talk show on BBC1, and Adrian was still plodding along as a long-term fixture on daytime TV with *Working Lunch*.

'Slow for the dough, don't play it fast, isn't that right, Johnny?' said Adrian to Vaughan. 'Who the **** are you?' said Vaughan, clearly genuinely perplexed.

A few more years later, and Adrian would be the big hitter, being paid the six-figure sums to do breakfast television, while Vaughan would be on London radio. It's a funny old world.

Back to September 1994 and that important man in Adrian's life, Paul Gibbs, the BBC TV head of business programmes and editor of a new project, a programme called *Working Lunch*. Gibbs wanted Adrian to be the anchor and so, despite widespread apathy verging on disapproval from the rest of BBC TV, that's what happened. Adrian remembers it well, and so he should.

'Paul didn't put me on air during my time at *Business Breakfast*. But that changed when he decided to launch *Working Lunch*. He'd auditioned loads of people for the presenting job, but apparently he had had me in mind from the start.

'Everybody, including various heads of BBC news at the time, thought he was stark raving mad. But Paul told them that, if they wanted the programme, he wanted Adrian to present it. That was a huge leap of faith. Paul staked his career on me doing *Working Lunch*.'

Adrian recalls the general reaction. 'If the rest of the BBC noticed at all, the standard response was "Who's this idiot?" It looked like it would fold by Christmas.' And then along came Victor Lewis-Smith.

At that time, the writer, practical joker, satirist and critic was probably best known for his BBC2 series *Inside Victor Lewis-Smith*, in which he played a patient lying in a coma in a BBC hospital for distressed broadcasters. His life-support system was plugged into a telly and a tour of his internal organs was punctuated with sketches of a bizarre and anarchic nature.

His earlier stuff, on Radio 1 for instance, had given Lewis-Smith a name for being objectionable, anti-Establishment and very unpredictable, and his column in the London *Evening Standard* as its regular TV critic was read as much for its forthright humour as its value as a viewing guide.

For some unknown reason, Lewis-Smith decided to review *Working Lunch*. He was clearly astonished by the presenter and penned the first of many articles in which he has attacked Adrian for not being very pretty. Likening him to one who, not having been in a road-traffic accident would still need to be identified from dental records, Lewis-Smith undoubtedly helped the new boy because, along with the insults, he did praise him as a presenter. Admitting to being in favour of ugliness on television, bearing in mind his own lack of loveliness, the critic gave *Working Lunch* the full quota of gold stars, including several for its front man's skills, attitude, good nature and so on.

Gibbs photocopied the review and sent it around the relevant in-trays. Whether it changed minds or not we shall never know, but certainly Adrian thinks it did some good with the waverers, and the show kept going, and Adrian kept going, not realising that he would be providing Lewis-Smith with copy for many years to come.

One of the reasons for his longevity, Adrian believed, was something originally perceived as a weakness – his accent. It seemed to lull great men into a false sense of security. They felt in no danger, being interviewed by someone who was obviously one of the lower forms of life. 'I'd ask a couple of dumb questions,' he says, 'then floor them with a third which showed I knew what I was talking about.'

Working Lunch was BBC2's business, consumer and personal-finance programme. It went out every weekday, 12.30 to 1pm, and was set up to be 'business journalism with a bite'. There was a lot of explaining of difficult issues in simple terms, such as what was really going on in the economy and, more importantly to the viewers, how that was going to affect them, in their jobs and as consumers. People could send in questions and have them answered by the experts.

In interviews, Adrian also aimed to ask the questions the viewer would want to ask, and had – quoted from the BBC – 'the unnerving ability to extract the maximum amount of information from his guests in the minimum amount of time'. There was also a conscious effort to be less starchy and formal than the traditional BBC business show. This was your nice, friendly bank manager rather than an editorial in the *Financial Times*, and your bank manager was from Birmingham. As one critic put it, Adrian Chiles was the BBC's token yokel, the man with the Christmas-cracker jokes.

At this point in his life, neither Adrian nor anyone else had heard the word 'blog', and the possibility had not yet arisen for anyone with a computer to call himself Knickersplitter, or herself Dickiedaidoh, and thereafter to spill any kind of rubbishy bile into the ether for themselves and folk of like mind to chomp over at two o'clock in the morning or, even worse, two o'clock in the afternoon (we use the word 'mind' in its loosest sense).

As no less an authority than Andrew Marr told his audience at the Cheltenham Literature Festival, 'A lot of bloggers seem to be socially inadequate, pimpled, slightly seedy, bald, cauliflower-nosed young men sitting in their mothers' basements and ranting.' Slightly unfair, we might say, but we get the point.

We have to wonder what Adrian might have felt, had he gone to see Gypsy Rose Lee and peered into the future – or maybe not. Even when young, not sure of himself perhaps, but more intelligent, sane and better educated than this lot, Adrian would surely have looked into the crystal ball and repeated the words of Clark Gable: 'Frankly, my dear . . .'

It's now official. Adrian Chiles is definitely one of Satans Slaves. And not the girlymen that like to dress up in leather and straddle a hot piece of metal. No, yer actual Satan and yer actual slave.

Because no sooner had I signed the Oxygen Intake Amendment Order/Form B12/12C (revised 6/09), officially cutting off all non-toxic gases from the odious, potato headed buffoon that is Adrian Chiles, he came on TV.

This man has the perfect face for radio, and the face only a mother could love. how can anyone pay him the amount of money that ITV are paying him for fronting the world cup shows on ITV. he knows next to nothing about footie, even i know more than him! there are more people about, ex football players etc, who know what they are talking about, he has no charisma. just please, get him off our screens. what do you think? please let me know!

Radio only with a gurning face like his and even then the graveyard slot for insomniacs and shift workers. His vowell problem is another minus. Then there's that grating personality. I think all fashion accents like his should be eliminated and a return to proper old school diction and pronunciation for news and current affairs shows. Paxman may be a pompous know-all **** but at least he talks total dead proper innit?

Ah, well. As is well known, there's nowt as queer as folk. That last comment could only have come from a dinosaur. The entire attitude to accents was changing. It wasn't a question of fashion, here today and gone tomorrow. Around the call centres, for instance, managers were realising that a posh Home Counties accent was not appropriate for someone answering a complaint. To most people, it sounded cold and distant. In the BBC, there were up-and-coming young presenters like Adrian, Welsh Huw Edwards and Scots Kirsty Wark who did not have to submerge their regional pride beneath newly reshaped vowels (or vowells).

It may even be the case that the pendulum had swung too far, and those whose regional accent happened to be Eton-with-plums were at a disadvantage. This was unfair. It was not their fault they sounded like HM the Queen but, to get on, some found that a compromise accent was necessary, with a touch of Jonathan Ross and a dollop of Thames Estuary. To much of the country this was even worse, but the BBC at that time felt that it was coming over as 'a little behind the sound of the nation; a bit antique'.

Working Lunch went out five times a week, middle of the day, 42 weeks a year, starting with a title sequence focused on a fish tank. In the tank were a rubber shark, a toy treasure chest and various other symbols of the City and industry, plus a real goldfish. Later this was changed to computer graphics, with the shark chasing the goldfish.

Naturally, the programme took a close interest in the Budget, and one year someone had the idea that Adrian should cover it from a pub in Birmingham. At Westminster, the BBC's main commentary would be coming from David Dimbleby (whose brother Jonathan is also a BBC regular). There was a technical rehearsal, and Adrian found himself chatting away to the great man, telling him that he was taking the opportunity to go along to watch West Brom that night. Dimbleby expressed regret that he wouldn't be able to watch his own team, Tranmere Rovers, who were engaged in a cup tie that same evening.

The thought was still with Adrian when it came to the live transmission the following day that he'd been talking football with David Dimbleby, and a David Dimbleby to boot who followed Tranmere Rovers, not something he could have imagined happening, but the business of the moment soon took over. He was waiting for the handover from Dimbleby, and here it came. And now, to Birmingham, where we're expecting to hear from Andrew Chiles.

'Thank you, Jonathan' was Adrian's response. Even as the words were uttered he felt his world beginning to fall in around him. Irate communiqués would be winging their way around the corridors of power, but there never was any comeback, apart from a few remarks on his quick-wittedness.

By 1998, things were looking up for Adrian. His proposal of marriage to Jane had been accepted and a date was set, and Radio 5 Live gave him his own radio show. Initially, to his considerable embarrassment, the show was called *Chiles on Saturday*, and it was for him to produce and write as well as present. It was a Saturday show, and it was Adrian, so football did tend to creep in a little – to the extent that the programme would win the Sony 2002 Sports Gold Award.

Adrian became known as a kind of people's champion. His dedication to football in general and West Bromwich Albion in particular, an affliction shared with his Brummie pal, the comedian Frank Skinner, was obvious to all. 'He's probably the only person who speaks like a normal human being about the subject,' said one listener.

His views on football were not technical, nor were they adulatory of stars as celebrities. He had grown up with football as the working man's sport, when players were paid well but not ridiculously, and when they were more likely to stay at one club during their prime years. Younger fans today, if they know their football history, will think of George Best and Bobby Charlton as Manchester United players and Bobby's brother Jack as a Leeds player. Best did go elsewhere while the other two didn't, but the point remains. Anelka? Er, who's he playing for now? Who thinks of Rio Ferdinand as a West Ham player?

In Adrian's youth, transfers happened, of course, but they made news. Managers generally didn't set out to buy a team. They bought judiciously, looking to strengthen where there was weakness. Mostly, they grew their own or bought very young, rather than shop for ready-mades in the supermarket.

It's impossible to go back to any kind of old days, good or bad, but it is instructive to modern football fans to think just a little about the way things were. For example, in 1904, an inside- or centre-forward (striker, if you must) called Alf Common was transferred from Sheffield United to his previous club, Sunderland, for £520, the first £500 transfer fee, and worth something like £200,000 today. Only a few months later, the same player was transferred to Middlesbrough, quite late in the 1904–05 season, for £1,000, again the first time a fee of that magnitude had been paid.

Yes, there was a lot of press coverage simply because of the £1,000, but the real issue exercising the minds of sports writers was the fairness of it, or otherwise. Middlesbrough were not doing well and were in danger of relegation. Was it right, everyone wanted to know, for a football club to buy its way out of trouble like this? Surely the honourable and sporting thing was to fight on with the team you had and, if it came to it, perish with stiff upper lip and firm jaw, rather than take a star off the shelf just because you happened to have a tempting amount of cash.

Whatever the sporting morals of it, Boro avoided the drop, much to the distaste and annoyance of those old-school types. Although that attitude has more or less disappeared now, except possibly in cricket, where people still grumble about overseas players being parachuted in for key matches, there remains a profound dislike of the notion of buying a football team, especially among those fans who have the misfortune to follow a club that can't afford to do such a thing.

Adrian's views on this, and matters surrounding, were often aired on *Chiles on Saturday*. On loyalty to clubs, he believed quite rightly that agents were at the heart of its disappearance. An agent gets no pay if a player stays where he is. Perhaps there should be a loyalty clause in contracts, so that the agent gets a regular commission if a player stays at his club. If the rules were to stay as they are, how could anyone blame an agent for making a deal the best way he can? Anybody would do the same. You can't expect club loyalty from agents: it's not in their best interests. Same with the players. Your Tom Finneys, who would never move because of that loyalty, are not around any more. Adrian says that, if he were a player, he'd want to earn as much as possible in a short playing life, and the clubs co-conspire by paying the money. If Man U pay £30 million, plus whatever wages, for Ferdinand and co., that influences all other wages and fees. Clubs are the first to say players get too much money and it's ruining football, but, when it comes to a struggle between such rival organisations for a particular player, all those good principles are forgotten.

The clubs, says Adrian, are tempted by money, just as the players are. The question is, if you are told a horse is a racing certainty at long odds, would you put everything on it that you have? That's what the clubs do. In order to win things, and so get vast sums of money, they bet vast sums of money on players who might help them do that. But they can't all win. A sensible fellow doesn't put his mortgage on a horse, but football clubs do the equivalent.

And the fans protest only after the act, says Adrian. If you ask a dyed-in-the-wool club follower, 'How do you feel about your club going into receivership?' that fan will say, 'No, of course not, what a disaster!' Phrase the question differently and say, 'Look, you could do with a better right-back and a top-rank striker. You can't really afford them but they could give you the edge for a European place next year. Do you think the risk is worth it?' What will they say?

Maybe the only way we'll learn is if a few of the really top clubs go bust, after risking too much. Football is a business, we can't deny that, but it's full of risks that other kinds of business wouldn't tolerate. Businesses have financial ambitions, and shareholders, and directors, and they are willing to take risks but, except for football, businesses take every possible step to minimise the fallout from risks as well as analysing the risks themselves. Too much happens at random in football for that to be true of football clubs.

Adrian has a point there. How many successful, well-run businesses would allow their fates to be ruled by incontestable decisions made by fallible outsiders, such as referees and linesmen, not to mention accidental own goals? If a mistake of fact is made in normal business, it can often be put right. If a referee says it was a goal, and it wasn't – think Thierry Henry and Ireland – there can be no review.

How many businesses are in direct conflict with each other, once or twice a week, on the battlefield? To exaggerate to press home the central issue, would shareholders have Tesco and Sainsbury decide their annual profits by holding a directors' golf match?

The rich get richer and the poor get poorer, in football as in life, and that's why, says Adrian, it will all end in tears. Already we know which clubs are going to make up the top half of the top division, and they want to stay there. That's why we never see anything of the so-called trickle-down effect. The top clubs don't want anything to trickle down. They only want it to trickle up. And it works, for them, for the moment. But the traditional football supporter thrives on uncertainty. Who is going to go to watch a foregone conclusion every week?

The answer, Adrian, we are very much afraid, is the

thousands and thousands who go to watch Man U, Chelsea, Arsenal and so on, because they do win every week, plus the thousands and thousands of children who live in Norwich, Brighton, Cardiff and Carlisle, who would rather have a Chelsea shirt for Christmas than one from their local club.

All right, says Adrian, here's another idea. You have the transfer window, or the transfer ban as some call it, which creates a similar situation to the old days: you start the season with the same set of players that you finish it with. There's talk of a wage cap, and of clubs having to live within their means. One way would be to do something like they do with baseball in America and even out the squads among the clubs. At the moment, the big ones could put out two entire first teams each, out of squads of 50 or more professional footballers. How can you expect Tranmere Rovers, or West Brom come to that, to compete?

What about sharing stadiums, Adrian? 'I'd set fire to myself outside the place if that happened.' And why hasn't Birmingham, unlike Manchester and Liverpool, produced a world-famous, trophy-winning side?

'I couldn't tell you. You can construct arguments about the whole city going through the doldrums, but that was true of Liverpool all through their success.' And those cities don't have three clubs almost in sight of each other. 'You could probably cycle from the Albion to the Blues via Villa in about 20 minutes. They're cheek by jowl.'

Could the Baggies win the Premiership in the next 20 years? 'Very unlikely, but that's the case for about 88 clubs,' Adrian thinks. 'You can't build anything. You need somebody with an absolute shedload of money, and even that's not a guarantee of anything, as Wolves have found. If you're talking about challenging at the highest level, then it's a fault in the system. You need to artificially create a level playing field. The FA don't have the will, the inclination or the imagination to do anything. Though, to be fair, they'd be eaten alive by the Premiership chairmen who *de facto* run the FA.'

Perhaps, Adrian, the balance will shift to managers, that special sort of manager who can make the best of the players he has. The trouble there is that such managers rarely seem able to keep up the success once they get the promotion. Any football fan can name such people who can make a silk purse out of a sow's ear, create fantastic team spirit, win promotion with a small squad of decent but limited players, then need to buy better footballers to stay up but don't seem able to hack it after that.

Every manager moans about lack of transfer funds. So, give a manager limitless funds and what happens? Success does not inevitably follow big spending. Look at Leeds and Portsmouth a few years back, and Man City more recently. Then you get people saying that such-and-such a team should go up because it's 'a bigger club'. What rubbish!

Adrian's idea of a good season is one in which some of the poorer clubs do better than expected. The stock market analysts could draw up a league table with the richest at the top, down to the poorest at the bottom. Then there's a choice. Award championships and prize money and TV money on the basis of that table, there and then, saving us all a lot of bother. Or play a season of matches. If the final table is different from the rich-poor table, give all the prizes to the poorer clubs who've done better than predicted.

During his summers of blissful relief from the worries of West Bromwich Albion, Adrian could mention the cricket on *Chiles on Saturday*. Indeed, he received the ultimate accolade in May 2005: the England squads would now be announced on *Chiles on Saturday* at 10.45am before each Test. BBC cricket correspondent Jonathan Agnew would come on the show with Adrian to analyse the selections and give listeners the first chance to hear from players in the squad.

But we get ahead of ourselves. Radio 5 Live and Adrian Chiles were becoming synonymous in many people's minds, and not just the sporty ones, and on 26 March 2004 there were just two days to go to Radio 5 Live's 10th birthday. All over the UK, it was noted, there were children of a similar age – the Radio 5 Live Generation. This was an opportunity that could not be missed. The 10-year-olds – the kids and the radio station – would meet for the first time on the eve of their 10th birthday at Alton Towers on Saturday, 27 March. Adrian Chiles would present his show, *Chiles on Saturday*, live from the theme park from 9am, and many of the children would be on the show to discuss the issues affecting 10-year-olds today, as well as the day's more general hot topics.

Then there would be a Radio 5 Live Generation photo, with children from Middlesbrough, Nottingham, Swindon, Aberystwyth, Manchester, Essex and Bedfordshire. These were all the children who contacted the station to take part in a unique survey of youth opinion, which aimed to reveal the thoughts, hopes and dreams of 10-year-olds. Quite what the thoughts, hopes and dreams of Radio 5 Live were at that point, we can't tell, but they must surely have included Adrian.

'Adrian's Saturday morning slot is a feast for sports fans ahead of the weekend's sporting events. What better way to wake up from a Friday night's hangover to the best show on Saturday morning?' said a spokesman for the radio show.

One of the side effects of top-level football being scheduled to accommodate Sky TV, plus the BBC's winning back of Premiership highlights rights in 2004, was a new BBC TV programme called *Match of the Day 2*, to go out on a Sunday night, to show and discuss the football taking place that day, review Saturday's goals and chat about soccer topics in general. Pundits would usually be ex-footballers with the occasional manager, referee or current player who had been involved in a Saturday game. It was important that the programme should be able to engineer an identity of its own, rather than be Episode Two of yesterday's show, and so a presenter was chosen who, the BBC believed, could do that.

Possibly, the great powers in BBC Sport were really canny, and made a strategic decision to give *MOTD2* a more cheerful, informal, less football-serious tone than that for which Gary Lineker was noted on BBC1. Possibly they looked around and saw a genial, self-deprecating, slightly pudding-faced everyman type, and thought, 'This has to be it.' Possibly they picked Adrian Chiles's name out of a hat or, most likely, it was something in between.

In any case, it was soon being billed as a light-hearted look at Premier League action, but whether the light hearts came before Adrian, or vice versa, we cannot say.

We can, however, say it was the change of gear that made the man's career. He loved his football but was not a technical expert. He could see the funny side of it from a distance, never having been professionally involved. If you want an opposite of Adrian Chiles, look no further than Garth Crooks.

Can you imagine Garth, or Gary, or any of them for that matter, asking a confused Gerard Houllier whether commentating on Liverpool for French TV was like watching another man sleep with his wife?

Adrian was known to radio listeners as a football man, but to TV viewers as a business correspondent and occasional introducer of documentaries and *Panorama* items that were nothing to do with football. He admitted to being worried. It concerned him that people might think him conceited or self-aggrandising. 'Who does this guy think he is? He can't be an expert on absolutely everything.' He may be a complete master of no trade but his image as the common-sense, common-man Jack of many trades is what has given him his popularity, with the common men and women in their millions and with those elite few who rule the common world. In fact, his first show attracted 1.9 million viewers, not at all bad.

The *quid pro quo* of being informal, slightly un-serious and cheerfully amusing is a lack of tight organisation and, as some apparatchiks, might see it, a lack of professionalism. Adrian may have spoken for the men and women on the terraces, and he may have criticised the influence in football of big money, and he may have been scathing about the prawn sandwiches and all the other indicators of corporate takeover, but he also soon acquired a reputation for being unusually prepared if West Brom had lost on the Saturday. Comments about the number of Saturdays on which this might happen are considered unnecessary at this point.

If it did happen, he avoided all other football results, *MOTD1*, and anything else to do with football until he went into the studio on Sunday lunchtime and had to face up to the inevitability of talking on television about something other than the national tragedy of West Brom's defeat. And there, in the corner, was a pile of newspapers with the scores in. He'd brush up that way.

Life divided between *MOTD2* and Radio 5 Live phone-ins could be difficult, for Adrian and for the people working with him. It was a Sunday job so, in the modern era when matches can be on any day and at any time that suits Sky, Sundays could also be West Brom days. That team playing on a Saturday meant no more in the great scheme of things than it would to any other husband and father obsessed with a football club, although it's always worse if you follow a team that keeps losing. Adrian would leave his wife and children and head for the Hawthorns and torture while other, less obsessed, fathers would take their families on a day out.

This was, after all, a man who would do anything for his team, anything at all. It's quite common for football clubs' matchday programmes to feature photographs of supporters wearing their team's kit in unusual locations. How many have had pictures of a TV personality in the buff? The West Bromwich Albion programme for a match against Arsenal showed Adrian posing with nothing on in front of two cranes in a dockyard, his dignity saved by a club badge in the right place. We have to ask: Dockyards? West Brom? Well, the Baggies won 2–1, so don't knock it.

On Sunday, in the *MOTD2* studio as he watched West Brom lose on the TV feed, knowing that he would have to talk about it later, it could be hell. For Gordon Strachan, with whom he presented the show in its first year, it could be almost as bad. Strachan is a bouncy character, never short of a sarcastic response to reporters' stupid questions. When asked, after a defeat of the team he managed, in what areas he thought the opposition had been the better outfit, he replied, 'In what areas? Mainly that big green one out there.' Asked if one of his players was good enough for the England team, he said he didn't care. He was Scottish.

Regardless of his natural buoyancy, he sometimes found Adrian's post-Brom depression a drain on his resources, and accused him in effect of being a carrier of infectious misery. Strachan had a point, and Adrian knew it, for example when he had to leave the TV studio to take the microphone for the Radio 5 Live phone-in. West Brom were drawing 0–0 with a few minutes to go. What would happen while he walked, or ran, rather, to his radio chair?

They have the same TV feed there, but the commentary is the radio one, which is moments ahead of the television. Adrian watched the opposition place the ball for a corner but heard the radio commentator excitedly report a last-minute winning goal. In the seconds before the TV pictures caught up, he had this wild imagining that the radio guy had got it wrong. There hadn't been a winner. It was all a mistake. But no, of course it wasn't, and West Brom had lost again, and the familiar agony swept over him, and the earphones were saying it was six o'clock, and time for Adrian Chiles to take your calls.

One big thing about him is his friendliness. He comes across as a chap you'd be happy to meet in the pub and have a few pints with, provided you could keep him away from the subject of West Bromwich Albion. The editor of the website football newspaper *When Saturday Comes* said, 'I'd like to put forward Adrian Chiles as the most likeable person on television. In fact, with Peter Glaze dead and Sweep not doing so much TV work these days, there are surprisingly few contenders.'

The editorial cited Adrian's ability to rub along with those pundits who are also friendly-seeming, such as Gordon Strachan. While certain telly experts might regard themselves as superior, for quite spurious and illogical reasons such as having played 500 games for Liverpool and 100 for Scotland while Chiles can only reminisce about breaking his leg in a five-a-side knockabout, bumbling Brummie Adrian still managed to muddle through and come out on the bright side. He also showed a rare interest in the players and referees as people, rather than as one-dimensional functionaries whose value could be described only in terms of what happens, or doesn't happen, when chasing a ball about a field.

'I think I pissed them off quite a bit when I started doing it because I didn't realise how hard it was. I had said to Niall Sloane, the head of football, "How much is there to it? If you're Des Lynam, it's money for old rope." It was arrogant; I thought I knew it all. You've got less room to shine just saying hello, and I didn't realise how bloody hard it is doing the analysis, going through the clips, on my part and the pundits'. I kept saying, "Let's have a look at that." The producer came in my ear and told me to stop saying, "Let's have a look at that." It makes you realise how brilliant Gary Lineker is.'

They all have their favourite phrases, don't they? Dear old Ray 'as far as the Premiership is concerned' Stubbs says, 'Let's see what that means as far as the Premiership is concerned.' Gabby Logan says, 'And now let's go to . . .' So 'Let's have a look at that' is no great shakes, as far as favourite sayings are concerned.

Of course, Gary Lineker's a pro, but not all of the football cognoscenti who came onto Adrian's show were pros. 'You're dealing with people who might not be that telly-literate. Tony Adams was absolutely hopeless at first, and he knew it, so he sought advice. Alan Hansen sits in the edit suite watching clips over and over again. He's the best for the same reason that David Beckham's the best at taking free kicks: he practises more.

'Gordon Strachan knows what's going to happen before it happens. One of the greatest experiences of my life was sitting on the sofa with him for a year and it all became clear. I'm normally very bad at reading the game. I can tell when we're playing well and I can tell when we're playing badly, but I couldn't tell you why.'

That's not why Adrian is there. He doesn't need to talk manager-speak about channels and holes and deep-sitting holding midfielders. He'd be happier if wearing the Number 11 shirt still meant you were a left-winger. Other football presenters such as Ray Stubbs and Gabby Logan may not be much better informed technically (although Logan, daughter of former Leeds United and England star

Terry Yorath, probably knows more than she lets on), but they don't have Adrian's clear identity as a fan, like other fans, like the fans watching the box.

Here's an interesting point, from Simon Hattenstone of the *Guardian*: 'Does anybody in the BBC sports department, apart from Adrian Chiles, remember Auntie's remit – to inform, entertain and, yes, educate? Believe it or not, television plays a role in nurturing future sports stars.'

And here's a response, a minority one, thankfully:

Frankly I'd rather they kept the quality pundits from the World Cup and dispensed with the Trisha style 'features' that seem to serve no function other than to pad out MOTD2 and remind us all how little football coverage the Beeb actually has. I know that there were only two matches on Sunday, but the limited coverage of the Man U match was just a joke. Chiles may recall the Beeb's remit, but that doesn't excuse him from being an atrocious presenter whose fawning comments make one long fondly for the days of Des Lynam.

And what about the Baggies, Adrian? 'I'm quite ill with it, really. I'm absolutely bloody obsessed. I never understand football fans who don't like the summer. For me, it's sheer bliss, the rest from worrying.'

And why are they called the Baggies? Nobody knows for certain. There are theories, connected with baggy shorts, bags of gate receipts being carried along the touchline under police escort and, most attractively, a story about the club falling into poverty so that the main players all left, to be replaced by lesser men. These smaller, thinner, less imposing fellows had to make do with the kit formerly worn by greater specimens, and so flapped around the field in baggy shirts and shorts. The game was much more physical then, and the best players did tend to be big and strong as well as skilful. Although this is not the most likely reason for the nickname, it is the one we most wish were true.

In 2004, Adrian was brought in as one of the judges for the *Guardian* Student Media Awards, with work experience among the prizes. Adrian's advice was simple: 'Aim high. I couldn't get a job at the *Solihull Times*. But I got one (on work experience) at the *Birmingham Post* and at the BBC. Once you're in, you're in. You might as well aim high because it's no harder to shine at the BBC than it is on the *Solihull Times*.'

In December 2004, the BBC announced that, from February 2005, it would be running a series copying (sorry, based on) Donald Trump's American hit, *The Apprentice*. It would feature Sir Alan (now Lord) Sugar in the place of the world's greatest comb-over. After a very successful run, they would do it again but this time with a little extra programme to go on BBC3. This is how the announcement was made.

THE APPRENTICE

Burning ambition meets the school of hard knocks in the hotly anticipated second series of *The Apprentice* – the show which sees 14 young high-fliers battle it out through a gruelling selection process for a year-long job with self-made tycoon and notoriously hard-to-please boss Sir Alan Sugar.

The 14 candidates face the biggest challenge of their lives – a 12-week-long job interview. Each week, their ambition, business flair and wit is tested to the limit as they compete in business tasks set by Sir Alan.

Divided into teams, the winners of the weekly assignment are rewarded, while the losers report to the boardroom for a showdown with Sir Alan and his two assistants, Margaret Mountford and Nick Hewer.

After being grilled on their mistakes, one is then singled out for the sack with the immortal words from Sir Alan – 'You're fired!'

Over on BBC THREE, viewers will be able to catch up with the latest firing after each episode of the series in *The Apprentice – You're Fired*.

Yes, that was it. One sentence, not even mentioning the name of the presenter. Perhaps they hadn't decided then. The mistake was corrected soon afterwards.

The second series also marks an expansion of *The Apprentice*'s regular programming and sees the launch of sister show *The Apprentice: You're Fired!* on BBC3, presented by Adrian Chiles (BBC2's *Working Lunch*).

The new show will give the fired candidates the chance to dish the dirt on their colleagues and provide their immediate reactions to the boardroom showdown.

The final episode will be followed by a one-off

BBC2 show *The Apprentice: You're Hired*, focusing on this year's winner. Adrian Chiles said: 'Each week I'll come face-to-face with the freshly-fired candidate who'll be spilling the beans on what it's really like trying to impress Sir Alan and, more importantly, what it's like to be on the receiving end of a boardroom showdown, and to hear the dreaded words – You're fired!'

At any rate, Adrian did the show in a satirical yet sympathetic way, with celeb guests, clips from the parent programme, comments from 'Srallan', and interviews with the failed apprentice, who always seemed a much nicer person than had come across on the show proper. Finally, the live audience were asked to vote, Fired! or Hired!, to see if they agreed with the top man's decision. In the *You're Hired!* one at the end, excellent ratings were maintained. After the hour-long *The Apprentice: the Final* at 9pm, Adrian interviewed the candidates and Sir Alan in front of a studio audience. The 30-minute show attracted 3.5 million viewers, taking a chunk out of Channel 4's popular *Desperate Housewives*.

After the first series of the spin-off on BBC3, the whole caboodle moved up a channel – *The Apprentice* to BBC1 and Adrian's show to BBC2, where it stayed. The show again gave the fired candidate the chance to reveal all on his or her back-stabbing colleagues and provide exclusive reactions to the boardroom showdown, and again the final episode of *You're Fired!* became *You're Hired!*, focusing on the winner.

Looking back, it would seem that *The Apprentice* was another pivotal moment in Adrian's career, equivalent to

MOTD2, even though, he says, 'It wasn't anything to do with me. I've got a disproportionate amount of the credit for it.'

Off screen he was busy too. Cited in one paper as 'Roly poly BBC presenter Adrian Chiles', he ran the 2006 London marathon in just under four hours, before going into the *Match of the Day* studio to show highlights of an FA Cup semifinal. His finish of 3 hours, 59 minutes and 42 seconds was quicker than the previous year, when he'd run dressed as the West Brom mascot throstle (which is an old term for a song thrush).

For some reason nobody quite understood – perhaps it was because he was not dressed as a bird – for 2006 he had been promoted from fun runner to athlete, which meant being taken to the start line in a bus with others holding the Elite Runner pass. 'I was sitting on the bus with Haile Gebrselassie, labelled an elite runner. I couldn't believe it,' he said. Nor, we imagine, could Haile Gebrselassie.

In mid-2006, Adrian Chiles could have judged himself as a great success – beyond his wildest dreams, to coin a phrase. 'I hate it when people say they've got a fantastic job. But I bloody have.'

He was football mad, and was fronting the World Cup highlights. He'd been doing *Match of the Day 2* for almost two years, *Working Lunch* for eleven-plus – which was one of the select few programmes to be featured on the new interactive, experimental BBC2 website with streamed highlights – and *The Apprentice: You're Fired!* had been going several months.

The previous autumn he'd presented a series of five episodes on daytime TV called *It Beats Working*, in which he looked at people who had successfully opted out of the nine-to-five routine that most of us have to live with. And most of us are working longer hours than ever before.

Olga Makharinsky was the woman who lunched, splitting her working day between shopping, the beauty salon and charitable events. Stuart Canlett was a househusband, a stay-at-home dad who looked after baby daughter Amy while wife and mother Becky carried on her career as an army officer. Tracy Shough did the camper-van thing around Europe, taking jobs here and there for cash and staying right out of the system, while Hector Christie had always known he would inherit a fortune and never have to work. Christie went on to higher things, when he dropped his trousers on *BBC Breakfast* to reveal a pair of underpants with a picture of Tony Blair on the front. It was apparently a protest on behalf of small farmers.

The year before, Adrian had done *Working in the Dark*, also for daytime, profiling five workers from a range of jobs, including the police and production-line workers, who keep Britain ticking over while everyone else rests. Some spend the night tidying up other people's mess and preparing the world for another day, while others keep watch, making sure that the darkness isn't dangerous, so we can sleep soundly and safely. Adrian endured daylight deprivation following five of these night workers from the moment they got up to the moment they went to bed. In an increasingly stressful world, he looked at how they managed to juggle work, rest and play in apparently difficult circumstances.

The first episode featured bin men in Glasgow, who demonstrated the techniques for sweeping the streets and steam-cleaning chewing gum off the pavements, and revealed how their shifts give them more time to spend with their families. The police episode was Adrian and two cops on a Friday night beat in Merthyr Tydfil. The Valleys town seemed calm, but the cops remained convinced there were no-goods up to no good somewhere. They just needed to find them. For the last in the series, Adrian met a couple who worked at the Rainbow casino in Birmingham, one on days, the other dealing cards through the night.

Adrian dealt evenly and amusingly with all these disparate elements, and he was similarly masterful with the cross-section of humanity that calls phone-ins, especially those whose subject matter related to football, such as 6-0-6, then at 10 o'clock at night on a Wednesday – and all this for a man who never imagined himself in front of a television camera. His ambitions to play in goal for West Brom – he being six-foot-one and therefore selected by his friends to play in goal in the school playground – had long been dismissed as fantasy. Becoming a television presenter never even got that far; it simply never crossed his mind. But, gradually, he had become a very widely recognised TV figure, not because he was the new Peter West or even the new Peter Dimmock, but because he was one of the lads. Well, one of the lads but not one of the anonymous lads. He's the one who cracks the gags, who leads without being the boss, who is brighter than most, and more likable than most, and yet remains equal with the rest, not seeming to want to stand out.

Mind you, he was clear enough in his opinion of England's performance in that World Cup, the one made notorious by the super-shopping, super-clubbing WAGs rather than by anything to do with football.

'I'm angry and frustrated. I would use one word to sum up the Sven-Göran Eriksson era: waste. It's one thing if you don't have talent at your disposal. But Eriksson had fantastic players. For the sake of everyone in every living room, every pub and at every big open-air screen, I wish that, just once, they'd won an effing penalty shoot-out.'

During that tournament he was asked to co-host a special edition of 6-0-6 with Prime Minister Tony Blair. To everyone except Blair, this seemed like a blatant attempt at bandwagoning. This was, after all, the politician who had made time stand still, or go backwards, by claiming he had been a regular at Newcastle United when Jackie Milburn was playing (the legend of Ashington, 'Wor Jackie', left the Magpies in 1957, when Blair was four years old).

As if that were not cringe-making enough, the PM also insisted that callers call him Tony. Older listeners were left imagining themselves saying 'Hi, Harry' to Mr Macmillan, or 'Wotcher, Clem' to Mr Attlee. Any listeners hoping for a loony to phone in, perhaps with some choice expletives, would have been disappointed because such callers were carefully screened out. Likewise, anyone hoping for a footballing revelation from the PM would listen in vain. He was far too clever to risk exposing his ignorance in trying to answer some question about the role of Emile Heskey vis-à-vis Rooney and Hargreaves, and would instead suggest unqualified support of the team.

Callers – and Adrian – could not ask political questions, but our boy never missed a chance to have a little dig. When asked if Beckham should play, the PM said yes, because there was nobody else who could cross the ball like him. Adrian said, 'But you must occasionally have had to lose someone from the Cabinet who can drop in a good dead ball?'

Blair's first World Cup memory, he told Chiles, was watching England's 1966 triumph while on holiday in France. Adrian should have regretted that the great win was a year before he was born, but could Tony remember if Jackie Milburn was playing? Instead, he underlined Blair's fundamental problem – public-school poshness in the Labour Party – by saying, 'In France? Wasn't that rather exotic for 1966?'

Politics almost appeared when Tone named David Miliband as the Cabinet's Wayne Rooney, and Tessa Jowell as Owen Hargreaves – as in taking a lot of undeserved flak – and football almost disappeared when he was asked why the Scots (not to mention the Scottish Chancellor of the Exchequer) were so reluctant to support England. He, the PM of the UK, could not understand why the Scots and the Welsh hated the England football team. 'As a Newcastle United supporter,' he said, 'I would be right behind Sunderland if they got into Europe.'

Leaving aside the likelihood of Sunderland getting into Europe, obviously dear Tone had only infrequently been to Tyne and Wear derby matches. Of course, if he had more of a regular, doubtless he would have thought that the things the Geordies chanted about the Makems, and vice versa, were only a bit of fluffy, harmless fun, as indeed are the everlasting curses laid on the English by the citizens of Jockadonia. 'I'm sure, Adrian,' he went on, digging his hole ever deeper, 'if Aston Villa were in a big

European final, you would support them, wouldn't you?' For once in his life, Mr Chiles was struck dumb.

Adrian Chiles on BBC World Cup TV was considered an all-round success, and not just for doing his job. There were memorable moments that could never have been scripted. For example, in the France–Portugal semifinal, the ball came up into the crowd towards Adrian, who jumped up from his seat and headed it back. Sitting back down, he said to Marcel Desailly, 'I've always wanted to do that.'

Throughout his football-broadcasting career, the occasional Colemanballs added to Adrian's laddishness, rather than pricking a hole in pomposity as it did with some. After Frank Lampard went to exchange friendly banter with the Kop, having scored against Liverpool, Adrian said, 'He's not the first player to go to opposing supporters with his lips across his mouth.'

Interviewing the Zimbabwean cricketer Eddo Brandes, known for his slightly portly figure, Adrian might have asked if it was true that Glen McGrath, annoyed at being unable to get Brandes out, had said, 'Why are you so fat?' To which Brandes replied, 'Every time I'm in bed with your wife, she gives me a biscuit.' No, Adrian didn't ask that. Instead, live on radio, he said, 'What was it like being a black man in a mainly white team?' to which Brandes replied 'Er, I'm white.'

Even his stunts left him still part of the gang, for example when he decided to do something about his famously hairy ears. He'd come across a depilatory cream that allegedly worked, so he invited the lady behind the product to come on *Working Lunch* and show the nation how good it was. In typical Adrian fashion he did this more or less on the spur of the moment, leaving producers and studio staff to sort out the problems when the woman turned up with her cream and began stuffing it in his ears. It removed the hair all right, at a cost of some pain, and it was displayed on a moderately serious business programme. Adrian could do that. He could do something silly, get away with it, still be an ordinary bloke, and still be the daytime voice of the BBC on business.

Victor Lewis-Smith didn't agree, of course. Having watched one of yet another of Adrian's many programmes, the first episode of *So What Do You Do All Day?*, he was particularly scathing about Chiles v. Branson. Seemingly, Adrian had allowed Richard Branson to use the show as a platform for advertising his wares, but that was only part of it. What really got Victor going was Adrian's face.

'Chiles has disturbingly piscine features, so much so that he makes Anthony Howard look like *Pop Idol* material in comparison.' While admitting that he, Lewis-Smith, is no looker and in no position to complain about others' supposed ugliness, he still found 'something unnerving about watching a programme presented by someone who looks like a sturgeon that's been prised into a bottle'. As we all know, caviar comes from the virgin sturgeon. Maybe that's where Victor got his Branson idea.

Another critic, the *Observer*'s Kathryn Flett, was much nicer about it. She thought Chiles slightly cheeky when he said, 'I've been reading so much about Richard Branson over the last few days – have you got any questions you want to ask me about yourself?' Even so, after a ride on a new Virgin train, a high-speed trip around the Virgin Megastore, another in a helicopter to

Virgin Atlantic HQ, and another down Memory Lane, Little Venice, where was moored the houseboat that provided shelter to the surging young Richard with his record shop on Oxford Street, Ms Flett felt that 'Chiles began to suspect that just maybe he was part of a typically Bransonian PR stunt'.

Surely, Adrian asked, there must be days in the life where it all goes wrong? 'I'm very fortunate that most days are fascinating and I meet lots of people,' said Branson, smiling that smile that could be genuine, could be warm and cuddly, could occasionally be the one on the face of the tiger that's the last smile you see.

When the subject was Derek Simpson, general secretary of the trade union Amicus, we found out that Mr Simpson liked Weetabix for his breakfast but hated politicians' soundbites and the privileges that come naturally to union bosses. The people's flag may be deepest red but so was that bottle of Premier Cru that went with the dinner at yet another restaurant no ordinary union member could afford. Such indulgence troubled Simpson, who remained convinced of the rightness of his cause, and the fact that viewers learned so much about him in a short half-hour was due, said a critic – not Mr Lewis-Smith – 'to the excellent Chiles, Barney Bear with a business-studies degree'.

In the ninth of the series, the 'ever witty and affable Adrian Chiles' had a day with Sean Doran, one of the world's biggest names in music and then chief executive of the English National Opera. Adrian told him that his first, last and only experience of opera left him 'bored to the point of dementia'.

Throughout all of this, he was always 'wanking on

about the Albion'. He covered for people on extra 6-0-6 shows and deputised on *Grandstand*. After two seasons of *Match of the Day 2* and many years of *Working Lunch* and *Chiles on Saturday*, a big change was coming, and we don't mean co-presenting *Sports Personality of the Year* with Sue and Gary.

CHAPTER FOUR

A LASS FROM COUNTY DOWN

In a neat little town they call Belfast,
Not meaning too long for to stay,
I there espied a pretty young maid
A-tripping along the highway.
She was most fair and beautiful,
Her neck it was just like a swan's.
And her hair it hung over her shoulders,
Tied up with a black velvet band.

All together now . . .

Her eyes they shone like diamonds,
I thought her the queen of the land.
And her hair it hung over her shoulders,
Tied up with a black velvet band.

Christine Louise Bleakley was born on 2 February 1979 to mother Mina and father Ricky, in the Daisy

Hill hospital, Newry, County Down. Newry is a large-ish market town by local standards and not far from the border with the Republic. Between the mountains of Mourne and the Cooley range, it stands at the head of Carlingford Lough, a sea inlet, by the Clanrye river, where St Patrick is supposed to have planted a yew tree to mark his visit and where a monastery grew that eventually became the town. Historically, Newry has had a considerable Irish-speaking population and, being close to the border, saw a sad share of the troubles.

The Bleakleys moved soon after Christine was born to Newtownards, main town of the Ards peninsula and only 10 miles or so from Belfast on the northern shores of Strangford Lough. This was generally a more peaceful place at the time, although not immune to the strife. Indeed, the largest car bomb of the entire troubles was exploded there in 1993, but otherwise the problems were minor and usually to do with feuding loyalist groups.

Christine's childhood was not disturbed and, as she grew into her teens, she made her first television programme. This is not a programme that readers will have seen, not even readers in Northern Ireland, and it was made some years before she had anything to do with the BBC. It was a chat show, called *The Bleakley Show*. After much badgering, Mr and Mrs Bleakley had given their pest of a daughter a small video camera, and said daughter set about directing, recording, producing and everything-else-ing the new show – everything, that was, except presenting. That she left to her younger sister Nicola, plus friends who were drafted in to give the weather and read the news.

'I asked for a video camera for Christmas one year so I

could record my own programmes and I'm not in any of them. You can just hear me bossing my sister about or whoever else I'd coerced into playing TV with me.' Presenting, being in front of the camera, didn't interest Christine half as much as being behind it (and ordering her sister about).

She'd probably never heard of Michael Winner, much less ever dreamed of appearing on a celeb cookery show called *Michael Winner's Dining Stars*. *Chris Moyles' Quiz Night*? Who's he? And one day, my dear, said the Good Fairy, you shall appear in a TV sitcom about a vicar. It will be only one episode, of a series called *Rev*, but the star will be on your own show, a show within a show as it were, with you and a fellow called Adrian . . .

Her own first leading role had her saying, 'What big eyes you've got, Grandma' as Little Red Riding Hood at her primary school, Castle Gardens. By the time GCSEs were top priority, at Bloomfield Collegiate, a private girls' school in Belfast, Christine was writing regular letters to BBC Northern Ireland at Blackstaff Studios, asking for work experience but not getting anywhere.

She sang in the school choir, performing madrigals at prize day, and was on Ulster TV's *School Choir of the Year*. Her A-level art teacher, Mrs Shearer, helped her with her studio ambitions and, through a friend who was a floor manager at Blackstaff, got her one day of unpaid skivvying at the centre of her fascination.

'Christine always had a smile,' Mrs Shearer said. 'Her only problem was her curly hair.' Unlike many of the other girls, she had no problem with boys. She didn't have a regular boyfriend until she was 18 and admits to being a late starter, in that respect anyway.

Actually, that first day at the studios, which also was her 17th birthday, was spent just staring goggle-eyed at all that went on. They sat her where an audience would be, behind the cameras, and there she was bewitched. Or, as she put it more formally, 'It was an exhilarating moment and only served to confirm my belief that this was the career I wanted to follow.'

They asked her back the next Friday to be the floor manager's slave, making brews, taking messages, doing whatever was required that a know-nothing slave could do. Christine, being Christine, developed this little opportunity. Soon, they couldn't do without her every Friday after school; and, when the summer holidays came, she was asked to take on paid work as a runner on a show called *Anderson on the Road*, with the experienced news reporter Don Anderson, who went on to senior positions in the BBC and elsewhere.

Being a runner means doing all the jobs that nobody else wants to do. You make tea for people who say they want it and then leave it un-drunk. You go out into the road in the pouring rain to direct traffic that doesn't want to be directed. You try to stop people walking across the shot when they don't care in the slightest about you or your silly programme. Senior people, and others who are too far up themselves, issue orders in front of you but indirectly, as in, 'Tell that girl to bring me a chicken-and-coleslaw sandwich on granary and a skinny latte,' when that girl is clearly visible at a metre away.

Even so, for someone desperate to get into television, it provided insight after insight into the way things work inside the industry. It was an apprenticeship without having a boss breathing down your neck – and without the risk of being fired unless you did something really stupid and irretrievable.

The next step up, from dogsbody/nobody, was to assistant floor manager. There's a parallel job in the theatre, assistant stage manager, usually filled by wannabe actors who are willing to trail around the country in touring rep, on the kind of money that assumes you can live off lentils, just because it's a way in, a way to get noticed, the bottom rung on the stairway to footlight heaven.

This was not the case with Christine. She had no ambition to be the focus of the camera's attention. Instead, she grafted, and got things done, and ran around with a clipboard carrying out instructions, all the time watching and learning on all sorts of different programmes. It was brilliant experience – 'And experience I still draw on today,' she acknowledges. For example, *The One Show* was a very wide-ranging programme that moved from subject to subject, demanding smoothly in-tune switches in style and tone from Christine. She'd seen it all at BBC Northern Ireland in many disparate programmes, so, when it all happened on *The One Show* in one half hour, she found it easier to cope.

Around this time, Bleakley was gaining some experience as a performer, reading the news and presenting programmes on radio, at the Belfast music station CityBeat, previously Belfast Community Radio. In 1998, her voice was heard on the (much underrated) film of Colin Bateman's novel, *Divorcing Jack*, as the local radio newsreader.

She left school as head girl, with A-levels in art, English literature, and government and politics, to begin a degree course in politics at Queen's University, Belfast, *alma mater* of such distinguished Irish folk as Mary McAleese (President of the Republic), Nobel Prize winners Seamus Heaney and David Trimble and the actor Simon Callow – but these are graduates. For Christine, the pull of TV was too strong and she gave up her studies after a year-and-a-half.

Floor manager was the next level and, as far as Christine could see, that was it. When she was given charge of the studio floor, the guests, the camera operators and sound engineers, when she was the one who was responsible for making everything happen, the director's amanuensis without whom chaos would reign, that was as far as she expected, or wanted, to go. This was the job envisaged by the producer of *The Bleakley Show* in that Newtownards back garden.

Looking back, there was also that reservation a straightforward girl like Christine might have after meeting famous people. Some are very nice, and some think they are God's gift. Fame can corrupt. For the yet-to-be-famous Christine, enjoying the camaraderie and team spirit of the studio floor and, don't forget, doing the job she had set out to do, the behaviour and attitude of some front-of-camera drama queens gave her no incentive or desire to become another of the same.

Then came the Irish Film and Television Awards. Christine was floor manager for the broadcast, the first time she'd done anything this big. Part of the job, whether it's awards, quiz shows or daytime nodding-off material, if there's an audience, it has to be addressed, in the manner of an air stewardess telling you how to operate your oxygen mask in the event of crashing into the sea.

The subject matter is equally riveting and the audience will pay just the same amount of attention as the airline passengers do, with the difference that a TV awards audience is invited and very probably half newted.

The other difference is that instead of a small crowd of ordinary folk, as might be for a typical studio programme, Christine had to give her fascinating speech – about health and safety, the format of the evening and miscellaneous other announcements and warnings – to 3,000 luminaries in various stages of illumination, in short, 3,000 of the great, the good and the tired and emotional.

Mike Edgar, the BBC's head of programme production for Northern Ireland, took note, and recognised someone who could deal with an audience. His first attempts at persuading Christine to change stations, from behind to in front, were rebuffed. She was flattered, and pleased to be asked, but no thanks. Edgar kept putting more and more bait on the hook, eventually coming up with a two-year contract to be a presenter with BBC Northern Ireland.

Christine consulted widely, with family, friends and colleagues. The general response was 'Go for it, girl', and so she did, knowing that if she failed she could always go back to being a floor manager. One of the great strengths of learning the business in a smaller environment is that you get to see all of it, all aspects of production, so moving in front of the camera for Christine was informed with that knowledge and know-how.

Her first regular show was an education programme called *Primary Focus*. There was a cookery programme too, *Spill the Beans*, and in 2001 Christine took a helicopter journey around Northern Ireland for her own show, *Sky High*. She took to the skies to view the beauty of the Ards Peninsula, flying from Slieve Patrick, via Strangford Lough to her own hometown of Newtownards, followed by the drama of the Belfast docklands and the heart of the city, revealing how the Northern Irish capital has developed over the years. There were four more episodes: the coast road to Fairhead and the Antrim Glens; the Kingdom of Mourne, visiting the Silent Valley, the fishing village of Kilkeel and the Norman splendour of Dundrum Castle; Sperrin mountain range; and finally the Newry Canal by helicopter, finding out what life was like for those who grew up in the area.

Not so long after her floor-manager speech at the Film and Television Awards, Christine found herself fronting a similar event, the Hot Press Irish Music Awards, held in the BBC's Blackstaff studios in Belfast, on Thursday, 25 April 2002.

The star-studded ceremony held in front of more than 500 invited guests was presented by comedian Patrick Kielty and Christine, to be shown on BBC1 Northern Ireland. It was a homely affair, with U2 winning three awards, the Corrs and their manager three, and Downpatrick's finest, Ash, winning two.

The weekly programme *First Stop* was another, a magazine programme that was partly an entertainment directory for the week ahead in Northern Ireland, plus 'things to do', co-presented with Ralph McLean. Christine was interviewed for a careers guide at this time, representing the job of 'Television Presenter'.

'The most important skills you need are being able to chat with people, keeping relaxed, and not thinking of yourself as the star. You must keep your feet on the ground. Of course you have to be confident, and be able to deal with pressure. Efficiency is another thing, like being able to cut a piece down to the required length in minutes and seconds, and ordinary office skills. You have to be able to type your scripts, because nobody else is going to do it, and see your scripts in terms of time on screen.

'Young people watch television and think that it's glamorous and glitzy and generally wonderful. Well, yes, it is, and a lot more than many jobs, but it also involves 15-hour days and standing out in the snow and rain and howling wind, while you make mistakes and the production team makes you do it again and again.'

She might also have mentioned having to get close to creatures that you don't really like very much. Christine has a well-known aversion to small furry animals and large feathery ones, so presenting a piece from Northern Ireland's World of Owls was a bit of a challenge. In the Randalstown Forest, what began as an idea in the head of a bus driver (Big Mike) has become a world centre for conservation, and Christine was so taken with it she became a patron.

'World of Owls and Wildlife Rescue-NI are active in conservation and education,' she said. 'They do a tremendous job bringing animal education in a fun way to all communities of Northern Ireland. I am very glad to be involved in these most worthwhile projects.'

Unwittingly foreshadowing certain events in the English Channel some years hence, Christine also had to conquer her fear of water, brought about by a childhood accident, by learning to surf. Her instructor was very impressed indeed when she stood up on the surfboard at the second attempt, but he didn't know how desperate she was to get out of that cold, wet, foamy stuff.

In 2003 she co-presented *Country Cool* with Ireland's favourite chat-show host, John Daly. This was an all-Ireland talent show for country-and-western singers, with a prize of a recording contract in Nashville.

Budding stars are being given the chance to be centre stage in a new search to find the next country music sensation.

A new BBC One Northern Ireland programme, *Country Cool*, is aiming to find an act with the potential to be the next LeAnn Rimes, Garth Brooks or Dixie Chicks.

The winning act will get the opportunity to record a single and album in Nashville to be released in time for Christmas.

Anyone aged between 17 and 30 on January 1, 2003, can enter.

The first round of auditions will be held in locations around Northern Ireland and the Irish Republic next month, with hopefuls being judged by local and international music industry figures and introduced by John Daly and Christine Bleakley.

One hundred acts who make it past the first hurdle will face more auditions in Belfast around the end of March.

Twenty-four finalists will take part in six heats which will be recorded in May and shown on BBC ONE Northern Ireland later in the year.

A panel of judges will pick six acts to go through to the final, with one extra act selected by a public vote.

US country artist Hal Ketchum will work with the finalists in master classes, and the seven acts will also receive training in all aspects of the music business.

The grand final will be broadcast live in the autumn.

Mike Edgar, BBC Northern Ireland's Head of Entertainment, Sport and Events, said: 'There is a massively rich vein of talent out there waiting to be discovered and we are really looking forward to bringing it to the small screen. It is also a fantastic opportunity for viewers to give some young person a well-deserved start to their career.'

Simon Cowell, eat your heart out! Christine's heart was in the papers, too, in Northern Ireland at any rate. Typical tabloid language told the good folk of that region that 'Gorgeous BBC presenter Christine Bleakley has told of her split with ice hockey hunk Curtis Bowen. But Christine, 24, says she'll stay young, free and single after splitting from the Belfast Giants favourite.'

The favourite of that moment was a Canadian, a six-foot-one attacking winger who had been prominent in the Giants' league and cup success. Quite why Christine had become cool towards him we are not privileged to know in detail, but she said at the time, 'Because of our jobs we were separated for long periods. He had so much he still wanted to do in the hockey world and I couldn't leave my job, either, as it was too important to me. So we were spending less and less time together and in the end it was just too difficult to keep the relationship going.

'There's so much more I want to do and so much more going on in the world that at the minute I don't have any time for romance. And next week I also start a new series of *First Stop* and as usual I'll be tearing up and down Ireland with my co-presenter Ralph McClean.'

She was also criss-crossing Ireland for *Country Cool*. 'We're down to the final 24 contestants and it will be up to the public to decide who will win the Nashville recording contract. The competition is tough. Whoever wins will become an international country star.'

As well as popular series, Christine was becoming the one to call on whenever there was a special event to cover. The Clash of the Celtic Giants started in 1999 as a Highland Games competition in Northern Ireland, and it grew into a massive crowd puller, attracting 40,000 people to the quiet north Antrim village of Glenarm.

In 2004 as always before, BBC NI TV covered the Games over two days, presented by Christine Bleakley and Stephen Watson.

Christine said, 'This was my third year of presenting the show and every year it just gets better. It's a really good family day out. It's a huge spectacle, particularly the women's events, when they lift cars and mighty trucks. The pure strength of those women never fails to amaze me, it's such a human feat. And, of course, the kids love it.'

Would you Pass the 11+? was a Wild Rover production and, in 2004, the first interactive TV event in Northern Ireland, hosted by Christine and Eamonn Holmes. In the studio there were 20 celebrity guests, all anxious to prove that, even if they hadn't passed at age 11, they could so now. Similarly, the audience was primed and ready, and folks at home could join in from the fabled safety of their armchairs.

Here are a few of the questions. You could not fail. The bottom 55 per cent were given grade D, the top 25 per cent A, but whether you would have got to grammar school or not – well, sorry, we can't say.

Science: Which of these creatures is not a mammal? Otter, whale, toad, elephant. Which of these characteristics do wood and stone have in common? Translucent, natural, synthetic, flexible. Which organ in the body co-ordinates all bodily functions? Heart, lungs, brain, face.

OK so far? Try sums. Fifteen is three-fifths of: 15, 25, 35, 9? 32 x 360 = 96 x: 1,080, 120, 36, 960? If a bag holds three red balls, three green, three blue and three white, what is the probability of picking, at random, one ball of any named colour? One to two (two to one on), three to four, one to four, four to one against.

English: Which word is incorrectly spelled? Decieve, apostle, quay, honorary. Which word is not a past tense? Done, wrote, learnt, saw. Which word has a different meaning from the other three? Error, joke, oversight, blunder.

All right, that's enough. Less taxing was *Town Challenge*, Northern Ireland's favourite game show, a local variant of *It's a Knockout* that had been running since 1997. When original presenter George Jones left in 2000, Christine joined it with Tom McDermott (*Big Brother*) and Percy the Parrot, to provide much-needed assistance to 'Uncle' Hugo Duncan.

The *Saturday Kitchen* cookery show, initially with Anthony Worral Thompson, then with host James Martin, had two famous chefs who, among other things, cooked a favourite meal for the celeb guest – another gold star for Christine. *Xposé* was a weekday, early-evening TV show, not unlike *The One Show* in concept, although more gossip/celebrity-inclined, on TV3, the all-Ireland commercial channel. As one critic noted, 'Ireland has a growing obsession with celebrities, not only in magazines, but across all media. With 68,000 viewers a night, TV3's *Xposé* is further evidence of our growing demand for celebrity news and gossip.' Christine, soon to be host of a show with 5 million viewers, was a sparkling guest for *Xposé*.

For two summers, Christine was co-host with Eamonn Holmes of *Summer Season*, another gentle, amusing, quirky kind of a road show, the magaziney sort of programme that so seems to suit Christine's style:

> Joe Lindsay looks at the reasons why Belfast is attracting an increasing number of tourists, Christine Bleakley examines the cost of getting married and Eamonn Holmes dons an apron to conjure up a selection of culinary delights with award-winning chef Michael Deane.
>
> Eamonn Holmes explores the coastline of Co. Cork and meets model Jamie Dorman, while Christine Bleakley takes in an aerial view of Northern Ireland. Joe Lindsey and Paul Rankin prepare strawberries.
>
> Season 2 Episode 6: Eamonn Holmes discovers the story behind the world's first safari park.

> Christine Bleakley offers advice on staying safe in the sun and Joe Lindsay catches up with the Farrell family.

Yes, well, you know the sort of thing. It works if the presenters are good. In 2006, there was *Big Bumper Science Quiz*.

> Join Eamonn Holmes and Christine Bleakley for popular science at its most enjoyable [said the publicity]. Beamed live from the W5 Discovery Centre in Belfast, and uniting the usual madcap capers of celebrities and keypads, this is a popular science quiz to tease and tickle everyone – even those without an 'ology' to their name.
>
> Playing at home couldn't be easier with online, Red Button, SMS and special playing cards to choose from and there'll be ample chance for everyone to take a breather when Christine wows us with wacky experiments designed to answer the most fascinating and bizarre scientific questions.
>
> With quiz rounds on everything from the human body to the sky at night, the craic will be mighty as our celebrities and you at home vie for the top spots and keep watching for the odd surprise or two.

Big Bumper Science Quiz was also produced by Wild Rover Productions for BBC Northern Ireland. Not everyone loved it – but do they ever? One irate viewer described it as a low-rent version of *Blankety Blank* crossed with the toddlers' channel CBeebies, which was a bit unfair to say the least.

It was around this time that Christine began going out with Mark Beirne, six years older than she, a Belfast businessman in the leisure industry and managing director of Life Inns Ltd. One day there would be talk of marriage.

One of the duties of celebrities is to present awards. Of course, Christine was adept at presenting awards programmes, but sometimes she was the one opening the envelope, as with the Deloittes Technology Fast 500 prizes in 2005, alongside Ardal O'Hanlon, the man who played Ireland's very own Craggy Island priest in sleeveless pully, Father Dougal, in *Father Ted*.

Another was when the University of Ulster played host to the Newtownabbey Volunteer Accolades. The awards, organised by the University's Knowledge Club and Newtownabbey Borough Council, recognised individuals and groups who volunteered in the local area. The ceremony was held at the University's Jordanstown campus and was hosted by Christine and comedian Gareth Fulton. Eleven awards were presented in total, including the University of Ulster Volunteer of the Year. Keep smiling, Christine, it comes with the territory.

Celebs, a category to which Christine certainly belonged in Northern Ireland by this time, also have to do things like switch on the Christmas lights and be the pretty face of local government initiatives. One such, in December 2006, was the Get Home Safe campaign, launched at one of Belfast's most popular nightspots, the Potthouse Bar and Grill. For readers who have never been to the Potthouse, but may go one day, there is a feature of which you should be aware.

Situated in the Cathedral Quarter, the Potthouse offers

pleasant contemporary cuisine made from locally sourced ingredients. It is a large, open-plan venue, on the site of Belfast's first pottery. It has a modern and spacious warehouse feel and features a glass ceiling, which is the dance floor of the Sugar Room club above. If you plan on moving upstairs for a dance, don't wear a skirt – or a kilt.

We trust Christine was suitably attired when setting going the Get Home Safe Partnership, led by Belfast City Council, in a bid to moderate the behaviour of revellers and 'improve Belfast's image'. She was also there to launch a new initiative, the Designated Driver Scheme, so we also trust she kept a straight face while listening to the following, from a council safety officer:

'The Designated Driver Scheme will complement the Get Home Safe campaign and is sponsored by Club Orange. On selected dates throughout December, drivers will be able to enjoy a free Club Orange.'

Yes, folks, on selected dates, you can have a free chocolate biscuit to help you get home safely. The rest of the message was more to the point. Christine advised those celebrating a night out on the town to 'stay in well-lit areas; don't become separated from your friends; never accept a drink from someone you don't know; plan your journey home in advance; always have enough money to get yourself home; don't walk through areas you are unsure of'. Sounds like good advice.

Just to show what can be the price of fame, look at this press release:

Red Bull launched a major creative contest today in Derry entitled 'THE ART OF CAN' with the Mayor of Derry, Cllr Lynn Fleming and TV presenter Christine Bleakley. 'Art of Can' is a province-wide hunt for creativity and is open to everyone, from full-time artists to simply those with a creative flare. There are no rules or boundaries other than the limits of the artist's imagination and talent.

Use the can and a little inspiration to conceive a work of art: a sculpture; a collage; piece of jewellery; a mobile; visual animation; a piece of furniture; a fashion accessory; a piece of modern art or something that no one has thought of before but make it beautiful, colourful, clever, amusing or outrageous. The only stipulation is that the 'Red Bull can' be the main raw material and the focus of the artwork.

A panel of three prestigious judges has been chosen and the works of art will be judged on creativity, conceptual idea and artistic standard.

An exhibition featuring the shortlisted entrants, as chosen by the judges, will be staged in the Guildhall, Derry from 28th April–7th May 2006. All shortlisted entrants will be invited to the exhibition opening night (27th April) where the judges will be presenting prizes to the three most extraordinary works.

Extraordinary indeed. And in the May of that year, the Belfast papers had a picture of Christine. It showed 'local personality Christine Bleakley' with Alan Rooks of Allied Bakeries, at the launch of the Modern Apprentice of the Year competition. The title, which Rooks lifted in 2005, was up for grabs to the top apprentice on the Department for Employment and Learning's Modern Apprenticeship programme. Christine was shown holding a tray of loaves of bread, dressed in white coat, white hat and red hairnet, still smiling.

Yes, and early the following year that game girl kept her smile while presenting a prize in a schools film competition to the winner in the category Best Use of an Animated Tortoise, and by the end of 2007 she was making a guest appearance in the long-running Northern Irish satirical TV comedy *Give My Head Peace*.

In between she had to wear more than £1 million worth of jewellery lent by Lunn's in Queen's Arcade, to host an entertainment awards show, where she was also being tipped to win Best Northern Ireland Media Personality. The embarrassment of having to present an award to herself was avoided when Colin Murray from Radio 1 won it. Then there was the Marie Curie Cancer Care Belfast Coca-Cola 7X Factor Event, very worthy, no doubt, but surely they could have come up with a snappier title, as did the Make a Wish Foundation Summer Event at Stormont.

Let Me Entertain You, co-hosted with the comedian Brian Conley, ran on BBC2 for two series of 20 shows each, between August 2006 and June 2007. It was a daytime talent show and, instead of Simon Cowell and co. telling the acts to get off the stage, it was the audience. Everyone had a voting button and, as the acts performed, gave them the yes or no. Once half the audience said no, the act had to go. A stay of one minute earned a £100 prize, two minutes £200, and the maximum of three brought £1,000 and a trophy. The best acts went through to the next stage. Any resemblance to Hughie Green's

Opportunity Knocks (BBC Light Programme 1949, Radio Luxembourg, then ITV with the famous Clapometer) was purely coincidental, similarly with Carroll Levis and his *Search for a Star* 'Discoveries'. Levis failed to discover the nascent Beatles, while Green claimed to have turned down Tony Hancock and Alma Cogan. As far as we know, nobody really special was lost to the public through failing at *Let Me Entertain You*.

'My career at BBC Northern Ireland started with filling the tea urn and ended, against all my expectations, in front of the camera,' says Bleakley. 'I will always recall my time there with deep affection. I loved the camaraderie and the close-knit atmosphere that permeated through the offices and studios, but most of all I relished the many opportunities that a regional department has to offer. By the time I left Belfast I had gained valuable and lasting knowledge of just about every facet of television production.'

As a result, the controller of BBC1, Jay Hunt, introduced her to the production team at *The One Show* and that eventually led the girl from Newtownards to all sorts of things she never expected.

CHAPTER FIVE

FAMILY AND FOOTBALL

If either party to a relationship comes into it with an all-consuming interest in something recreational, whether it's beekeeping, amateur dramatics, dahlias or following a football team, it is bound to affect that relationship in some way. It might even be responsible, wholly or partly, for terminating it.

Before Adrian Chiles fell for Jane Garvey, he had been engaged to another, and he took this young lady to a football match. Looking back, perhaps a quiet-ish sort of home game, a mid-table, end-of-season kind of thing, without much riding on it, would have been the ideal. Unfortunately, West Brom are not always able to provide a mid-table position at the end of the season, and so it was that Adrian and fiancée travelled to Portsmouth, to see a game that West Brom had to win to avoid relegation to the third tier of English football, then called League Two, nowadays called League One, and if you can make sense of that you must work in marketing.

It was 8 May 1994. Ayrton Senna and Roland Ratzenberger had been killed a few days before at Imola. The Channel Tunnel had opened, Nelson Mandela was about to become President of South Africa, and Tony Blair was soon to become leader of the Labour Party following the death of John Smith.

Matters like the South African elections and the dangers of motor racing may have been mentioned on the way down to Fratton Park, home of Portsmouth FC, but if they were it was only to avoid the mental anguish that would surely follow any discussion of West Brom's chances of a win. Portsmouth (nicknamed Pompey), although safe from relegation, were no great shakes, with 58 points to West Brom's 48, but a reasonably good home record. Still, there was hope. Or was there?

Travelling to the match were thousands of rabid West Brom fans, nigh hysterical in their anxiety. If any of them thought that, well, their team had played badly all season and so deserved to go down, just as much as the other candidates – Peterborough, Oxford and Birmingham City – they didn't give that impression in the stadium.

Adrian's girlfriend – fiancée, rather, his proposal having been recently accepted – obviously knew about him and West Brom but, like so many non-sporty girls, believed that it was just a phase he was going through. She knew that, after 'wed' had been 'locked', he would grow out of it. Or perhaps she just thought it wasn't all that important. Only a game. That sort of thing.

If she did believe it was only a game, a few minutes among X thousand West Brom fanatics soon changed her mind. The atmosphere was manic, maniacal. Mental derangement characterised by excitement and

Adrian and Christine at the BAFTA television awards in 2009.

Above left: Christine celebrates with Karen Hardy, one of the professional dancers on *Strictly Come Dancing*, at the opening of her new dance studio in London, 2008.

Above right: Pictured with Gordon Brown after crossing the English Channel on water skis in aid of Sport Relief in 2010.

Below left: Christine at the *Glamour* Woman of the Year Awards in June 2010, flanked by Piers Morgan and Amanda Holden.

Below right: On holiday in Sardinia with Frank Lampard.

Above left: Adrian at the Television Sport Awards, 2004.

Above right: Adrian looking reasonably happy at a West Brom match… although the game hasn't started yet.

Below: Pictured in 2007 at the London Stock Exchange with Alan Sugar and other members of *The Apprentice* team.

hallucinations. A vehement passion, a range, a craze. All those things. How could she be expected to understand?

When West Brom scored, every maniac suffered derangement, and sheer agony for the rest of the game until the ref blew his whistle for the end. Their beloved team had survived for another season in the second tier, then called League One, now called the Championship, and when that new season started it became clear to the fiancée that West Brom was not a phase Adrian was going through after all. She broke off the engagement.

Things were different with Jane Garvey. Jane was already a football enthusiast. Brought up on tales of Ian St John, Tommy Smith, Ron Yeats and Bill Shankly, she was not alienated in the slightest by a visit to Carrow Road in April 1996, to see West Brom go 2–0 up only for Norwich to pull two back and get the draw. At the start of the following season, Adrian couldn't get to the game at QPR but Jane went on her own and watched from behind the goal among all the Brummies. Two–nil to the Albion, and Adrian knew he was going to have to marry this girl.

Later, with family interests competing with football, Jane's view would change. Her husband's marginally bonkers devotion to the cause prevented too many normal things from happening. He was accused of selfishness, immaturity and lots besides. When she made a joke about the marriage vows, that 'in promotion and relegation' should be inserted between richer/poorer and sickness/health, she was being humorous only to a very limited extent.

They were married, with normal vows, in Swansea in 1998, when Jane was undoubtedly the better known of the two broadcasters. From being the first voice heard on Radio 5 Live in 1994, she had gradually moved through the day, to the midday slot, also presenting *Everywoman* on the World Service, and then to the *Drive* weekday afternoon show.

Jane was on the Swansea train that crashed at Southall in 1997, killing seven people, and filed impressive news reports from the scene on her mobile phone. Daughter Evelyn (Evie) was born by Caesarean on 18 December 1999. West Brom were at Ipswich. If they won, and Jane had a boy, it could be called Cyrille. Fortunately for the poor child, she was a girl, and West Brom lost, so there was no possibility of calling her Cyrilla.

Adrian once described his very talented wife as 'the small, angry woman who presents *Drive* on Radio 5 Live'. For a good part of their relationship, pre- and post-marriage, Jane was the more prominent broadcaster of the two. Had family responsibilities not taken first place, BBC prophets would have expected her to become one of the biggest names. Nevertheless, if the story is true, Adrian might have become a bigger name sooner, had he accepted the offer of the Radio 5 Live breakfast show, supposedly made to him in the summer of 2002. At that time, Adrian was described as 'a sports and business presenter with a distinctive Midlands accent'. Contrary to other reports that give him as someone unable to turn work down, he is alleged to have asked for a four-day week to spend more time with his family, and BBC Radio wouldn't do that.

Regardless of uneven profiles, there was always a certain amount of interest from the public in their private lives, and Jane was always most adamant that nothing should ever intrude in any way that would involve the children. So, just to prove it, this happened. Adrian had parked his car at the Hawthorns and was walking towards the stadium when a man shouted to him.

'Hey, Adrian,' he cried. 'You'll never believe what your wife just said on the radio.' Adrian had to go over to find out. 'Er, what?' he asked, cautiously. 'Someone on the programme asked her if we were going to win promotion. Guess what she said.' Adrian, of course, couldn't guess although he could imagine a few things. Jane was keen on football, but there was a difference that she could see, which maybe Adrian couldn't, between liking it, being a fan of it, and being obsessed by one team playing it. For Jane, being married to a West Bromwich Albion disciple was like a steak-and-pie lover being married to a vegetarian who did all the cooking.

'Go on, tell me, put me out of my misery.'

'Yeah, well, she said she flaming hoped not, because last time they went up she had a baby nine months later.'

That was younger daughter Sian. Adrian, not sure if this was an expression of his wife's wish to limit the size of the family, or a comment on his wild-animal behaviour after West Brom glory, continued to his seat, in hope rather than expectation, perhaps glad that Jane hadn't mentioned his wedding present to her: a West Brom season ticket.

It is illuminating to examine the roots of this word 'obsession', a word used too lightly too often. If we look at what it used to mean, we can begin to see just how applicable it is in Adrian's case.

Our word obsess comes from the Latin verb *obsidere*, to sit down before (in front of, not in the sense of taking turns), and its main meaning originally was in religion. It was said that when an evil spirit took possession of a person, that is, haunted or beset that person, the poor victim was obsessed. To obsess also came to have a meaning in warfare – to besiege or beset a castle or town.

An obsession was when the devil, or another malevolent force, set in motion this haunting or besetting. Gradually the meaning mellowed, and we can do no better than quote the modern meaning from the *Shorter Oxford Dictionary*: 'Obsession: the action of any influence, notion or fixed idea, which persistently assails or vexes.'

Listen. You can almost hear Jane Garvey, Mrs Chiles, saying 'Hear, hear!'

An influence, a fixed idea, persistently assailed Adrian – and quite frequently vexed him – and, to judge by the vexing that took place when he sat down in front of West Brom and they lost, it can only have been an evil spirit that started it off, and not his granddad at all. His friend and fellow Baggie man, the comedian Frank Skinner, is equal in devotion but always looks on the bright side. His hope springs eternal. He says things like, 'At least we lost to a good team.' Adrian, on the other hand, is like the hypochondriac (which Adrian admits to being in his youth) who goes to the doctor, and the doctor tells him there's nothing wrong. Obviously, the doctor is incompetent.

When West Brom are 2–0 up with half an hour to play, Frank Skinner sees three points and another win at the next game. Adrian sees the opposition scoring twice, and winning through an own goal in time added on.

An early goal for the Baggies has Frank beaming with

delight. Adrian will look glum, sure that it will make his team overconfident. One difference between many fans, what you might call 'ordinary' fans, and these two – plus others such as ex-prime-ministerial adviser Matthew Taylor and Simon Darby, gardener, conservationist and former deputy leader of the British National Party – is that they, the high-profile ones, are not supporting to give themselves an interest in life. They are not looking for a way of being part of something, for an identity above and beyond the mundanities of ordinary existence. They already lead extraordinary lives. They don't need the aggro of the blue-and-white stripes to give them something to laugh and cry about, to make them feel as if they are, after all, important.

Maybe Adrian, and others who have made an impact on the national consciousness but who remain human, need the heartbreak of a moderate football team to give the ego and the emotions a friendly knock from time to time. Those ordinary fans, who manage to scrape along without fame and fascinating variety, perhaps find that their lives don't stretch them enough. They don't want a life without extreme highs and lows, so they follow the Baggies.

Of course it's not all bad. Take, for example, the sight of the glamorous women Adrian observes, those who attend the games when West Brom travel to London for a midweek evening match. These dolly birds clearly know nothing about football, but their current gentleman callers are West Midlands born and bred, West Brom fans dyed deeply in the wool, and these young men-made-good-in-London have brought their arm candy with them to the game at, say, Chelsea or

Fulham, with the promise of a few drinks before and a nice dinner afterwards at a fashionable restaurant.

The girls settle in their seats, impressed with the colour of it all, the pageantry, the lights, the sound, and then the teams come out. All around the pretty ladies, West Brom fans arise and rain their own special blessings on the opposition players, and the boyfriends join in the obscenity and wrath. How can this be? How can the aforesaid gentleman caller, perhaps a fellow doing well in the City or an advertising agency, who knows his way around wine lists, who takes his girl for weekends away at country hotels, be mixed up with this foul-mouthed gang of half-drunk, working-class robots, all chanting in unison concerning private matters that hardly bear thinking about?

Later, over the Dover sole and Chablis, the boyfriend might defend himself and his fellows with talk about the native wit of the working man. What about the time, he might say, when Man U put the long-haired blond Diego Forlan on as sub, and we chanted 'One Sally Gunnell, there's only one Sally Gunnell'. No? Maybe not. You had to be there, really.

In December 2005, Adrian was offered three free tickets to a Christmas carol concert on the day that West Brom were away to Portsmouth. Let's take a vote among dads with young children. If you had the choice between a carol concert with the kids at the Royal Albert Hall, no less, and an away football match with the distinct possibility of losing, which would you go for? Yes, we thought so. Which did Adrian go for? You know the answer to that. Don't ask. And if that was followed by Man U away on Boxing Day? You might go to that, like

Adrian, having given a solemn undertaking to your wife that you would never again attend a football match on Boxing Day, so long as ye both shall live.

There were other rules, too, set by Jane, and these were rules to be kept. In the event of West Bromwich Albion's losing, there were to be no grim looks, no snarling at the children, no grumpy responses to innocent questions. Of course, such a rule would not be a problem for those who follow football teams that usually win. For Adrian, it meant digging into deep reserves of acting talent that he never knew he had. And, in consolation, he could sympathise with fans of successful clubs. They would never know the joy of victory as he did, because they were used to it. They would never know the despair of defeat as he did, because they knew that, if they did lose, they would win next week. It's like that joke about people who don't take a drink. When they wake up, that's the best they're going to feel all day. Or the philosophical observation that, to experience the joy of promotion, one must first be relegated. When Adrian goes to a match, it's in expectation of seeing his team lose – so, when they do win, or fight back from behind for a draw, he is HAPPY.

Psychologists might say that it is the combination of the worry, the dread and the hope that is actually worse than the event itself. All season you labour under the threat of relegation – or, if you follow Man U or Chelsea, the threat that you might not win the Championship or the European Cup. When your team does, or doesn't, do what you've been hoping for or dreading, what happens to you? Nothing much. You might get drunk. You might shed a few tears. You might conceive a child, admittedly, but that would be rare. Otherwise, life goes on.

One time he watched West Brom concede a last-minute goal to Fulham after playing well enough to win. He went on 6-0-6 with the words, 'Call me quick before I do something stupid.' Jane had Radio 5 Live on while she was giving their two daughters their bath. Evie, the elder daughter, took things literally as young children will.

'What's Daddy going to do? What's Daddy going to do?' she cried. Jane calmed her and waited for Adrian to come home.

'That earned me a hearty bollocking. Richly deserved, I have to say.'

So, who are these people, news of whom can send Adrian's heart rate up almost as high as one of his regular long jogs? Who are they, for whom Adrian feels the unconditional affection that is normally the preserve of dog for master? Of course, the dog expects food, water, shelter, walks, stroking, the fulfilment of pleasing its master and the opportunity to be a dog, and it doesn't know any better or different. None of that applies to Adrian Chiles, although, as the dog cannot control the master except indirectly, by inspiring love and respect, so Adrian cannot control the object of his untrammelled dedication. So, we ask again, who are these people?

They were the West Bromwich Strollers to start with, a team with its foundations inside the factory that made Salter's scales and spring balances. This was in 1878. The team had a strip – white shirt and shorts, maroon stockings, blue cap with red pompom, and blue sash – but no ground. They changed in a pub called the White Hart (now gone) and played on a field at Cooper's Hill, on which now stands St Phillip's Church. They had goalposts but the crossbar was a tape, as was common then. A couple of years later, the Strollers seem to have amalgamated with another West Bromwich team, called the Albion, and assumed that name, or it could have been more of a simple name change, with some of the players coming from the Albion district of West Bromwich.

Association football was going through a period of evolution at this time. The star players of old were the dribblers, the ones who could make long runs past lunging defenders, before shooting at goal or perhaps making a short pass to an onrushing colleague. The dribbler had to be careful about this: passing forward without three opponents between him and the goal meant that his colleague was offside. Naturally, nobody had thought of the offside trap. That would have been considered most unsporting.

By now, dribblers were gradually disappearing as the emphasis switched to coordinated team play. Competition was getting hotter. Men were being paid to play, but the code of the amateur still ruled. Basically, this could be summed up as: breaking opponents' legs was fine, but there was to be no cheating; and you had to appeal for a goal, like cricketers appealing for a catch or LBW.

Here is an extract from a match report from West Brom's first Cup final, 1886, against Blackburn Rovers. They had drawn the final tie proper, at Kennington Oval, 0–0, and the replay was at Derby, on the cricket ground.

Rovers, now with Walton in for Heyes, led at half-time with a goal by Sowerbutts, scored after twenty-six minutes as a result of a raid in which Walton and Fecitt were prominent. The same player again beat Roberts, but the Rovers players made no

appeal for a goal, thinking him offside. Later it
transpired that the referee would have been willing
to allow the goal to stand, as Sowerbutts had been
played on by an Albion defender.

Albion, with their famous rushing tactics, fought
like demons, and constantly harried Arthur in the
Rovers goal. At a time when Albion were striving
hard for an equalizer, a memorable goal by centre-
forward Jimmy Brown clinched victory for Rovers
with seventeen minutes to go. An Albion attack
broke down and Brown collected a pass from
McIntyre well inside his own half, and suddenly set
off on a run for goal. He dribbled past man after
man and at last slipped the ball between the Albion
posts for a wonderful individualist goal.

Imagine! The Rovers players made no appeal for a goal
because they thought it was offside.

In 1888, a chap called William McGregor, a Scottish
draper with his business in Birmingham, wrote a letter to
12 of the strongest (in his view) football teams, all in the
North and Midlands, suggesting they band together to
form a league. His main reason was the lack of firmness
in friendly fixtures, which was all they'd had until then
apart from cup competitions. Teams would cancel or
postpone friendlies for their own purposes. With a
league, the teams would be committed to a fixture list for
the season.

McGregor was a director of Aston Villa, who had
beaten West Bromwich Albion in the 1887 English FA
Cup final, the middle one of three finals for West Brom;
they would win the third against Preston North End.

There was still a strong connection with Salter's: the team were mostly amateurs, mostly working at the factory. Rovers and North End were notoriously professional, however. Preston even committed the heinous crime of importing players from Scotland to play in England, for goodness' sake!

So the Football League was formed, and West Brom were founder members, with their professional players on 10 shillings (50p) a week, the equivalent of about £250 a week today. West Brom won their first game 2–0 away at Stoke, and finished reasonably comfortably – won 10, lost 10, drawn 2. There was no relegation then. There was nowhere to go, which was just as well in the 1890–91 season, because West Brom finished bottom.

Here is the world's first ever association football league table, 1888–89 season:

	P	W	D	L	F	A	PTS
Preston North End	22	18	4	0	74	15	40
Aston Villa	22	12	5	5	61	43	29
Wolverhampton Wanderers	22	12	4	6	51	37	28
Blackburn Rovers	22	10	6	6	66	45	26
Bolton Wanderers	22	10	2	10	63	59	22
West Bromwich Albion	22	10	2	10	40	46	22
Accrington	22	6	8	8	48	48	20
Everton	22	9	2	11	35	47	20
Burnley	22	7	3	12	42	62	17
Derby County	22	7	2	13	41	61	16
Notts County	22	5	2	15	40	73	12
Stoke City	22	4	4	14	26	51	12

Attendances were generally around the three and four thousand mark, except for cup ties, and friendlies were still played, for example against Newton Heath, which became Manchester United, and Small Heath, which became Birmingham City. The rest, as they say, is history, with one league championship (1919–20), five FA Cups and one League Cup (1966). The Baggies have been relegated nine times, the first in the 1900–01 season and, of course, promoted nine times, the first in the 1901–02 season. Without some very extensive research, it is not possible to say if this puts West Brom at the top of the list of uppers and downers, but they must be close. Perhaps Adrian should switch to Blyth Spartans. They've never been relegated – although they've been very near to it a couple of times. Maybe not, then, Adrian.

Not that he and Frank Skinner are the only media personalities who are also Baggies addicts. There's Peta Bee, of the *Guardian*, for example. She's not very keen on some aspects of crowd behaviour.

My season ticket at West Bromwich Albion has me sitting six or seven seats to the left of someone who spends the entire 90 minutes on his feet, singling out one player for abuse at decibels that give me tinnitus.

Usually it is our midfielder Sean Gregan who is the subject of his attack; the thickness of his thighs appears to be a source of great irritation to this chap. 'Uh-oh, here he wobbles,' and 'Send fatty to Weightwatchers, Megson,' are two of his choice phrases. It would not grate so much if he did it through despair, but he is the same when we are 2–0 ahead.

Clearly I am not alone. Radio 5 Live's Adrian Chiles, who sits in front of my dad's mate in the next row, threw down the gauntlet to fellow Baggies fans recently by challenging them to provide examples of supporters who display the most annoying vocal habits during a game.

Last week's programme featured a sample of what can only be described as an outpouring of emotional tension that has clearly been simmering since August. To give you a taster, one fan sits a couple of seats from someone who is forever standing up, arms outstretched, taunting the away fans until they catch his eye, at which point he gives them a two-fingered salute.

And that's not the half of it, Peta.

There can be no doubt that Adrian's West Brom fixation had a negative effect on his marriage, but that wasn't the whole story by any means. The balance of work also came into it, and what that meant for the children. During Jane's 13 years with the evening *Drive* programme on Radio 5 Live, she and her co-presenter Peter Allen won six Sony awards, but, by 2007, with the girls needing more and more of Mummy's attention, Jane scaled back her work activities and began presenting *Woman's Hour* on Radio 4 in place of Martha Kearney. Such a move did not go unnoticed by Radio 5 Live fans.

I was saddened when Jane Garvey left Drive for BBC Radio 4. But Peter Allen and Anita Anand do a great job of hosting this show. The interviews are well conducted and there is a lot of humour in the show. Peter Allen always talks about his vegetarian daughter and his love for Tottenham Hotspur football club.

Anita has made an incredible career progression over the past few years. I used to see her on Zee TV in charge of heated debates. She then used to appear on the Chiles on Saturday show. Subsequently she hosted a late evening weeknight show on Radio 5 Live. I love the various anecdotes from her life. Once she arrived home in an angry mood, she took off one of her high heels and threw it at the wall causing damage. One New Year's Eve her brother's pet snake had coiled itself to the TV/VCR wires and she spent 3 hours trying to untangle it.

Yes, well, it was much funnier at the time, but our thanks anyway go to a chap called Mr Paella.

Jane's move to *Woman's Hour* had a mixed reception. Zoe Williams, no less (the *Guardian*, if you didn't know), called her a misogynist after Jane wondered aloud if women in their hearts really wanted the top jobs. Jane herself put family first, and laughed off the criticism, quite rightly, on the grounds that Radio 4 is a prime generator of angry letters from a vocal minority. The majority, from her own experience, thought she was good at her job, and especially those she was brought in to attract: the younger ones. Men make up a third of the audience for *Woman's Hour*, and Jane certainly appealed to them, but there was a job to do if the programme, and the channel come to that, was going to survive against TV and the internet. Women with young children had to listen, if there was to be any hope that those children might turn into listeners too.

Adrian, meanwhile, was taking on more and more work. Some say he couldn't say no. Some say the various magnetic fields of work, family and football pulled him about too much, and he allowed the wrong ones – work and football – to pull him too far away from family. Jane's magnets were the kids. 'Adrian is a very successful television presenter and it makes no sense for me to demand to work five or six days a week. I now have the best part-time job in the world. It's interesting, challenging, and I can pick the kids up from school.'

His popularity was not lost on ITV, who tried to poach him with a long-term, multi-million pound contract, but he stayed loyal to the BBC. If 'friends' and 'sources' are to be believed, this would be the only time he ever refused an offer of work, apart, possibly, from the four days he wanted for *5 Live Breakfast*.

When the couple announced their separation, more 'friends' suggested that it was Adrian's ambition that was to blame. Despite maintaining that all of his career beyond straight journalism was an accident, and defining ambition as a dangerous thing, Adrian's work ethic was given a different slant.

'He likes working, but also feels he has to say yes to everything' is a comment attributed to Bob Shennan, Adrian's former boss at Radio 5 Live. 'I think that has caused some people, not least his wife, some exasperation.'

'He decided that he could be bigger. I think he got a bit grand,' said another 'source', because Adrian had decided he needed a better-known, harder-hitting agency to represent him at his new level of success.

Although absolutely everybody, including the two principals and all friends and sources, denied that anybody else was involved in the breakdown, the gossip media tried to dig something up on Adrian and Christine, but their mutual admiration did not imply romantic association leading to divorce proceedings and a new life in *Hello!* magazine. Possibly, gossip writers can never accept the truth when there's a possibility of a 'Beauty and the Beast' scoop, or rumour, or wild imaginings.

The split between Jane and Adrian happened before the football tournament Euro 2008, when Adrian was widely praised as best presenter in the BBC's coverage, but the news was kept secret for a while. Perhaps Adrian should have taken more note of that show he did in 2004, *Working in the Dark*. Quote: 'In an increasingly stressful world, he looks at how they manage to juggle work, rest and play in apparently difficult circumstances.'

Adrian, then aged 42, was divorced in 2009 by Jane Garvey on the grounds of his unreasonable behaviour. He has admitted he would like to find another partner in life, preferably an intelligent woman but not necessarily a beauty. 'Divorce is a very private thing and you don't want people to write about it. It's one of the worst situations life can throw at you, but I haven't given up. I just want someone to take care of me.'

Ladies forming a queue should bear in mind that his relaxed, charming, unruffled, humorous personality, as revealed on the telly, is not all there is. 'I'm very temperamental. Whenever I get mad, I think that's the Croatian part in me coming out.' Ah, yes, those temperamental Balkan folks, they can be a bit of a caution.

Another side of him is his faith – not in West Brom,

except in the sense of the old definition: faith is believing in something you know to be untrue. No, his Christian faith is lifelong and has become more intense with his conversion to Catholicism, a process that requires a great deal of instruction and, in Adrian's case, a spiritual commitment above and beyond the previously necessary attendance at West Brom's matches.

'I've always wanted to grow out of the football obsession. It hurt that much when I was 12 to see Albion lose, but I thought that it wouldn't feel so bad when I grew up. Wrong again.'

Looking for a serious method of sorting out the real hurts in his life, Adrian spent many an hour talking about the Bible with Sister Jennifer, and having deep conversations with Father Ben, a priest whose speciality was the chronically ill, 'people pegging out and turning to God,' as Adrian put it. 'I asked him whether that tested his faith, and he just said that a thousand difficulties don't add up to one doubt.'

Adrian had been thinking about becoming a Catholic for years, so he went to Mass and that did it. 'At my first confirmation class, the priest said I'd have to do every Tuesday night with Sister Jennifer, and I thought, "Will this be the moment when I walk in and realise it's a load of nonsense?" But she's everything I dreamt she might be, a lovely woman full of goodness, but not in a pious way. We have a laugh. And she watches *Match of the Day 2* out of loyalty.'

Another aspect of Adrian that future partners should bear in mind is his cooking. He can do it. He can make gnocchi. If he weren't so busy, maybe he'd be on *Celebrity MasterChef*. And he knows a bit about wine, too.

Whoever is in the aforesaid queue, it won't include Christine. They really are just good friends but, at that time, whenever they were spotted together, more denials had to be issued. Of one incident, when they were seen going into a private residence, Adrian said, 'It looked suspicious but it was totally innocent. Rather sweetly, in the reporting of that they were absolutely accurate in the timings. If they had said we had got in at 8pm and left at 3am, we could not have disproved it, but we were in there for 52 minutes with two mixed kebabs. And if anything else was going on, would we have bothered with the mixed kebabs? As anyone I grew up with would tell you, if anyone was capable of getting Britain's most desirable woman into an empty property and do nothing but eat kebabs, I am that man.'

Adrian and Christine talked about the rumours. She said that people seemed to have given up for the time being. He leaned over and said, 'That's because they've realised you're not good-looking enough for me.'

Christine felt sorry for the photographers, saying, 'I thought, "They're going to be bored stiff, hanging about for nothing." My life is dictated entirely by my work. Every day is the same. The most exciting scoop they got was Adrian buying a takeaway. He said, "Christine, I'm going to have to hold my hands up to the nation and say: I like kebabs. I know saturated fat is bad for you, but I do." He's fun to be with. A funny man. And all the photographers and rumours, it all goes with the job. It's not something I had to manage in Belfast.'

The gossipmongers went mad anyway. Piers Morgan said that Adrian was the only man he knew who could be incarcerated with Christine and be more interested in his dinner. Christine confirmed it. 'It's all complete nonsense. I didn't even eat a kebab. He had them all.'

A newspaper persuaded them to take part in a Mr and Mrs quiz, to see how well they knew each other. Favourite food? Said Christine, 'We went to a French restaurant and he ordered fish, chips and mushy peas.' Correct answer: fish and mushy peas. Said Adrian, 'She eats like a bloody horse. It's fantastic to watch. There's nothing left. It's like the fox has been at the chicken coop. She'd have a big pork chop.' Correct answer: lamb cutlets with mint sauce or a pork chop.

They got each other's favourite song right, too, and shoe size, but fell down on pets. 'I've got no idea if Adrian had any pets. Sorry,' apologised Christine.

'We had eight cats that were all called Mitts,' explained Adrian, 'and Christine befriended a neighbour's dog that died.'

'My mum told you that story,' Christine said. 'He was called Benji.'

Asked to save something from a fire, Christine rightly picked anything to do with West Brom, while Adrian went for her hair straighteners, saying, 'They'd probably have started the fire.'

Adrian said he'd been through every emotion since being romantically linked with Christine, from anger to embarrassment to flattery and now boredom. 'One paper ran a story about me giving her a lift to the airport. They had pictures of her with a suitcase and a handful of hair straighteners. That's how banal they can get. And she was going on holiday with three guys off *Strictly* [*Come Dancing*]. Why didn't they make something of that? They never let go, do they? She comes with me to help me buy something at the shops, and that's proof we're living in sin.'

In one way, Christine didn't mind the fuss. It allowed her to, 'Go out with other blokes,' she said. 'If I'd been with Adrian the papers would have made something of it.'

And, added Adrian, Christine had fixed him up with a couple of blind dates with her friends but nothing had clicked so far. 'With us, you've got a standard beauty and the beast. Old grey bloke, attractive younger woman. Rough-looking blokes like me can get on telly when rough-looking women can't.'

Christine said, 'Would I be sitting on the sofa with him if I was as ugly as him? Probably not, but a brain is also required. Isn't it, dear? You see, with TV couples, the story is either they detest each other off screen and their show is an act for the cameras, or they're bonking in the green room. The middle ground, which is the truth, is that we just get along. When the rumours first started I went through the angry stage. Then I thought it was funny. Now I'm like him – it's boring. Our relationship is a bit of a love-hate, brother-sister thing. It's taken a long time to get to that stage and it's not going to go any further.'

When it was revealed that she had split from her boyfriend of three years, Mark Beirne, in January 2009, there was more smoke, but still no fire. Denials of a romance continued as the two presenters were seen together on a number of occasions, such as when they left a hotel by the back exit at 1.15am after helping to introduce the *Royal Variety Performance*. At last, the smoke blew away.

CHAPTER SIX

THAT LONG
SLOW CAREER

It was in the autumn of 2000 that the unsung heroes of *Working Lunch* found themselves fashionable. Previously hidden away in a cardboard box at the back of a BBC News broom cupboard, presenting a show watched only by pensioners, night-shifters who couldn't sleep, idle students and other pizza-eating riffraff, Adrian and Adam's snip-snap half-hour of money news was largely unappreciated inside their employer's organisation. It was, as they say, below the radar. It was a business and finance programme in the middle of the day. Did boardrooms and offices fall silent, as everyone from MD to office boy settled down around the company telly to be instructed by Adrian Chiles? Probably not. Therefore, given that the audience must have been the previously defined riffraff, it was a programme about business and economics for those parts of the population who were not in business and didn't really affect the economy much. If the BBC were to follow this scheduling

127

plan to its conclusion, they would put *EastEnders* on at five in the morning and *Blue Peter* at midnight.

Or was it a gallant attempt to make intrinsically difficult and boring subjects, such as economics, interesting – nay, even entertaining – to daytime viewers? Would Lord Reith have been proud?

The BBC News Department was all about politics. Well, almost all. The folk at the top seemed to think that what went on in Westminster and Washington was of the utmost interest to normal people, in that it affected their lives minute by minute, whereas normal people have always been much more interested in their own ability to get along, and what they might do to improve that ability. There's a Northern expression questioning the relevance of something: What's that got to do with the price of fish? News bosses may not have known what this meant, but *Working Lunch* did.

And then the great man himself, Greg Dyke, saw the show, liked it, and included it in a speech to the Confederation of British Industry. He extolled the virtues of the presenters Adam Shaw and Adrian Chiles. He used the word 'innovative' to describe their slightly eccentric (by traditional standards) style, more to do with the absence of jacket and tie than pinstripes and watch chain, shirtsleeves rather than stuffed shirts. Subject matter, too, was not what everyone might expect. How do firms selling Christmas hampers make their money? What are the economic pros, cons and difficulties in running a chippy?

The business world according to Chiles and Shaw was not entirely centred on London. By 'innovative', Greg Dyke may also have meant not London-centric, and, when it was London, not the capital as normally seen through the eyes of the BBC.

In any case, Dyke wanted more business in the news, and he wanted a new one-hour edition of *Working Lunch*. The problem they had on the programme was largely forced on them by their midday slot, when big business wasn't watching. A large audience of small investors did not enthral industry and finance big hitters, and they wouldn't come on the show. As Adrian said, the banks, the great financial institutions, even the Financial Services Authority (FSA), set up in the first place to be on the side of investors, all were deeply reluctant to comment for *Working Lunch*. New start-up businesses, on the other hand, clamoured for a mention.

To illustrate that catch-22 is alive and well, the programme was criticised by business people because it didn't run for 52 weeks a year, therefore the BBC was un-caring of business, which is why the big names would not appear, and Chiles would only take the mickey, anyway. Well, the highest authorities in the BBC had decreed that *Working Lunch* should not interfere with coverage of important sporting events, such as the tennis from Wimbledon, the Olympics and political party conferences.

When he did get the FSA on the show, Adrian found their spokesperson less than forthcoming. The FSA was seeking a different way for some financial products to be advertised. Ads for pensions, for instance, trumpeted performance in the past, which is no guide to the future. Warnings about investments going up or down did not get much prominence in the sales chat, understandably. So, how was this revolution to be brought about? Adrian wanted to know.

Well, the FSA would write letters to the advertisers. Which advertisers? Ah, we can't tell you that. 'You won't name and shame anyone – why not?' asked Chiles.

'It's not the role of the FSA to name and shame' was the response. Oh, wondered Adrian aloud. So whose role might that be? Well, you see, that's really the sort of thing that the media and consumer champions do. Adrian had clearly been labouring under the misapprehension that the FSA, formed to be a consumer champion, was, in fact, a . . . Oh, never mind. Here's a picture of a goldfish.

Not long before Christmas 2000, Adrian Chiles was described as a 'financial journalist' but one who, jocularly, was not terribly competent himself when it came to finance. In particular, contrary to the message in more recent TV ads, he found tax returns to be taxing.

'My accounts are in good order,' he said, 'but it takes time.' Like many freelancers, anxious to minimise their income tax (or at least not overpay), but equally fearful of being accused of wrongdoing, Adrian found the paperwork daunting. 'I spend as much time on my receipts as I do on the work that produced them.' That, plus letters from the accountant and general uncertainty about money, made him much more appreciative of those old PAYE days. 'I'd gladly pay 40 per cent rather than fiddle around with all this.'

Hmm, yes, maybe, but the freelance way of life is a balance. Adrian admitted he earns lots, but he has no job security. 'They could sack me tomorrow.'

Otherwise, he was no different from many young men with their eyes on the future. Proving that old saying about the cobbler's son being the worst shod, he spent all week talking to the British public about money and ways to look after it, but did very little along those lines himself. It took the arrival of his daughter Evie earlier in that year to start him being sensible, contributing to a pension, putting cash into savings, and taking out life insurance.

He and Jane also took the decision to stretch themselves as far as they could in buying a spacious family home in Shepherds Bush. They had to bridge to get it, and the experience made him work-hungry. The loan seemed huge to the boy from Hagley, brought up when houses were priced in tens of thousands, not quarters of millions, and he would do anything going if it meant he could get that loan down.

He was never a big spender, anyway. An ordinary Ford saloon, holidays at his parents' Welsh cottage and his grandma's Croatian one, his season ticket for West Bromwich Albion, golf and home cooking – these were the simple parameters of his private life.

There was, though, the time he simply had to fly to France for a football match. Croatia, a new team playing for a new country, had beaten Italy in Sicily in 1994 while qualifying for Euro 96, and they reached the quarterfinals of that tournament. The 1998 World Cup, in France, would be a sterner test.

Adrian happened to be in Canada for Croatia's quarterfinal against Germany, so he watched it on big-screen TV in Toronto with, it seemed, a thousand Croatians out for a Saturday night. They won, and the semifinal would be against France on the Wednesday. Adrian was back in London by the Monday. Paris wasn't far away. He just had to go. A Croatian journalist friend got him a ticket. They met in Montmartre for a liquid lunch that extended well into the afternoon. If the match was going to be a memorable occasion, it did rather look as if they wouldn't be able to remember it.

On the way to the game, Radio 5 phoned Adrian's mobile, wanting an interview. Mum was on air as well and so they had a chat in Serbo-Croat, with Adrian's fluency much improved by his lunch-aided lack of inhibition.

The first half went by in a blur, 0–0, and Adrian needed the toilet. He queued for the whole of half-time and was still queuing when Davor Suker scored for Croatia. Adrian was back for the French equaliser soon after, and their winner with a desperate 20 minutes left to play. The French were down to 10 men but held on. Another disappointment, but still a victory of sorts for a nation only recently reborn.

The cottage in Croatia was his mother's, an old stone house in Tisno, on the island of Murter in the Adriatic, a tiny place joined to the mainland by a bridge, landing you on the coast between Sibenik and Zadar.

To quote the local tourist office,

Tisno is the most authentic place in the Murter island where is still possible to find the old stone houses and typical Dalmatian narrow streets or some original *konoba* with good wine, salt fish and Dalmatian ham. During the stay in Murter island it's strongly recommend to visit the Kornati National Park (archipelago) – daily excursions have been organized from all places. It is also possible to hire an boat (even with skipper) and choose an route by yourselves (in the summer is necessary to book the boat in anticipate). The island central position and connection with the coast facilitates the visit to other Dalmatian attractions: waterfalls of river Krka, Sibenik, Zadar, lake Vrana but it is more probably that the beauty of Murter, their bays and pine woods will keep you on the island for all holiday time.

Or, as Adrian said, the cottage was on an ancient stone street going up a hill, and they went there most summers. The island is small and hilly, with several beaches. He says he usually ate a hundred figs on his way back from the beach, which is a mile or so, then completed his five-a-day with a half-pint of *slivovica* plum brandy.

Adrian backed up the official description, too. It is indeed more probably that the beauty of Murter keep you on the island, if only for the views rather than the local wine. You have a panoramic view from the top and, out towards Italy, there are the uninhabited islands (Kornati), an incredible sight on a moonlit night.

Brother Neville and Adrian had a dinghy with an outboard motor, which they used to go around the islands. Alas, being an inflatable, it died from an un-mendable puncture, leaving Adrian with a dream. 'When I'm a millionaire, I'll buy a proper boat and take us all to those fantasy islands.'

As a financial journalist, on his way to a million, possibly, he felt obliged to invest in the stock market. Readers who know something of that subject may like to form their own opinions on his portfolio, which at the end of the year 2000 consisted of Leeds Sporting (the parent company of Leeds United), BT and Marks and Spencer.

'Everybody at the BBC bought M&S thinking they couldn't go any lower, but they did. Maybe that was because we waved a pair of M&S knickers about on *Working Lunch*.' He didn't say what everybody at West Brom thought about his owning shares in Leeds United. In early 2001, there were rumours of a new venture for Adrian. According to various sources, a BBC presenter was being recruited for a new version of Channel 4's *Big Breakfast* show. The presenter in question was Adrian Chiles, described as currently the host of the BBC2 business-news bulletin, *Working Lunch*, and BBC Radio 5 Live shows, *Chiles on Saturday* and 6-0-6.

If the rumours were true, nothing came of it, but it did show that Adrian's star was rising, one consequence of which was a chance to present *Sunday Grandstand*. It was also an opportunity to assert his Brummagem heritage, with a link from the tennis in Birmingham to the rowing in 'the marginally less fair city of Seville'. These programmes are scripted, but presenters like Adrian will ad lib if they feel like it. If the following line was an ad lib, it was a very confident one. If it was scripted, by an enemy or Adrian himself, it asked a lot. On the subject of golf and Tiger Woods, Adrian said, 'Tiger's on fire ahead of the competition he's never been on fire for before.' Shades of 'Forfar Athletic five, East Fife four'.

Meanwhile, life went on, with *Working Lunch* and the Radio 5 Live sports shows. One Saturday morning, Adrian had someone in the chair who professed an addiction similar to his own: Alastair Campbell, the spin king, who loved Burnley FC. At the time, Burnley were doing well and looked as though they might get into the play-offs for a Premiership place.

Everything went swimmingly until Adrian sprang a little surprise. While the sound was away playing news and weather, he told Campbell that he proposed to do a miniature version of the *Mastermind* specialist subject, and ask him three obscure questions about Burnley FC. Campbell went bananas and threatened to walk out, so Adrian quickly read him the questions. Campbell answered them all swiftly and correctly. When they came back on air, Adrian announced the Great Fan Test and asked three 'very difficult' posers, which Campbell, playing to the audience, laboured over but got right in the end. As he would.

Not long after that, Adrian had some bad news for his listeners. Former West Brom and England striker Jeff Astle died, collapsing suddenly at his daughter's home. Astle, 59, scored the extra-time winner against Everton in the 1968 FA Cup final, which Albion won 1–0.

He had come from Notts County in 1964 and became one of the Baggies' greatest players, scoring 137 goals in 292 league appearances. He won his first England cap in 1969 and was in England's 1970 World Cup squad in Mexico. He played five times for England but never scored.

Adrian said supporters of the club would be shocked at the news. 'He was a natural goal-scorer. In front of goal, there was nobody better. For every West Bromwich Albion supporter in the world, the world stands still the moment we hear he's gone. He was a fixture at the club. He was there week in, week out. He was part of the substance of the club. It's a great loss.'

Quite early one morning in May 2003, the BBC opened its bleary eyes after a rather strange dream. In this dream, a tall, un-athletic, shambling kind of a broadcasting chap with a genial, easy way of prising secrets and describing events, not to mention getting some fun out of unpromising subjects, suddenly handed in his cards. This was a surprise, but not as big a surprise as the number of cards he had in his hand. It seemed that this fellow had been hosting the BBC2 programme *Working Lunch* for nine years, and the meal before that, *Chiles on Saturday* at breakfast time (ish), and the Radio 5 Live football phone-in called 6-0-6, and he'd been on *Panorama*, *Grandstand*, *The Money Programme* . . . Who was he?

It happened that, at the big meeting scheduled every day at the BBC, at which those Very Important Persons who have thick carpets in their offices discuss yesterday's shows, a documentary item presented by this shambling, genial chap came up for discussion. It was all about the Chanel fashion house and, in particular, its perfumes. A man worked there called the Chief Nose, and his job was to sniff samples of perfume all day long, in the form of a drop on a piece of filter paper.

The interviewer had turned this into a brilliant slice of TV, much impressing two of the top types, Lorraine Heggessey and Jane Root. Heggessey was controller of BBC1 at the time, and Root controller of BBC2. We can perhaps excuse these busy ladies from not having listened to football phone-ins, and maybe they preferred Radio 3 to football on a Saturday morning, and maybe Ms Root was always working at lunchtime, but plenty of BBC insiders were highly amused at the way the tall, shambling et cetera broadcaster was suddenly the bee's knees, so much so that the two top ladies were fighting over him.

Root wanted him for *So What Do You Do All Day?*, a series in which a reporter would trail around after a famous celebrity squillionaire for a day in the life. Heggessey offered him quiz shows. Meanwhile, Radio 5 Live is said to have asked him to be the host on the breakfast show. Then there was the offer from *The Money Programme*, and more *Panorama*, and more sports programmes. Channel 4 had a go, and ITV, but the BBC was home, and had been all this time, where there was variety.

The BBC2 version of *The Money Programme* had Adrian conducting a special investigation into the Football Association. BBC2, 7.30pm, money – what sort of an audience could they expect? How about 1.2 million? Very nice, thank you.

In August 2003 he fronted a rather personal documentary on BBC2 called *The Colour of Friendship*. The idea was to examine his own attitudes to race and colour, in a serious but Chiles-ish way, and thus apply what he found to the world in general. He noted that all of the 130 guests at his wedding had been white. Not a brown, black, or any kind of a non-white face among them. Looking back, this seemed shocking.

'I reckon I'm a nice, liberal kind of guy, living in London, so why are none of my friends black or Asian or Hispanic or Chinese?' The metropolis, he recognised, was about as multiracial as you could get. If any countries on this earth were not represented, it would be very hard to name them. So, was Adrian, unknown to himself, prejudiced in some deep-vein, secret, born-with-it way, or were society and his life incompatible, so that black and white paths never crossed?

He travelled from his Shepherds Bush home to his West Midlands beginnings. While wishing, liberally, that the pop song 'Melting Pot' by Blue Mink would somehow come true, he could only come to the conclusion that, as in the words of Muhammad Ali, bluebirds fly with bluebirds. People naturally gravitate to their own kind. On the programme he went to a Nigerian wedding and journeyed with Britain's only entirely Asian coach company. He met up again with the only black lad there had been at his school when he was there. In the words of one critic, 'There was nothing hugely insightful or intellectually profound about *The Colour of Friendship*, but Chiles was an endearing guide.'

'Endearing' isn't perhaps the word Adrian might have wanted to describe his *Money Programme* report called 'Viagra: The Hard Sell' on BBC2. Versatile, confident in his abilities, able to cope with a programme that seemed to be one long double entendre – those words would have been more apt than endearing, thank you. 'The Hard Sell'? According to Adrian's investigation, there was no need. The world was stiff with men wanting help in the trouser-snake department; they just hadn't said anything about it. So, voicing over film of skyscrapers, fountains, and balls going down holes, Adrian told us that Pfizer discovered by accident the cure we didn't know we needed for the dysfunction we didn't know we had. The researchers had been looking for a cure for angina, but the volunteer triallists reported increased heartbeats for different reasons. And now, young men take it even though they don't have a malfunction, while out clubbing on amphetamines. So that's what 'speed dating' means.

Around this time, Adrian gave up his Saturday morning Radio 5 Live sports programme, an event that attracted the fury of that doyen of sports writers, Frank Keating. He accused the BBC of gormlessly dumbing down its 9am Saturday sports potpourri, 'from Adrian Chiles's discerning and crafted medley of recent years to the present discordant ego-tripping teenager-touting tripe'. And you can't say fairer than that.

There were TV documentaries, such as *Royal Millions*, a 60-minute investigation into the wealth of our first family, concentrating on HM the Queen and HRH Prince Charles. Special reports on European food wars and banking were done for *Panorama*. This was all good, career-enhancing stuff. Perhaps not so well advised was Adrian's venture into 'acting', in a Johnny Vegas vehicle.

This was a cinema film probably made with the late-night teenage and pub-chucking-out-time DVD market in mind: *Sex Lives of the Potato Men*. The main male characters are linked through their profession – selling potatoes around the fish-and-chips emporia of Walsall – and their pursuit of intimate encounters with female lady persons, with varying degrees of success.

Reviews in newspapers and magazines were universally terrible, often emphasising the shock-horror of rubbish like this getting a million quid of Lottery money:

'At least Chubby Brown has some vague notion of innuendo. This doesn't have the wit to stagger to the end of the pier.'

'Mackenzie Crook has an unfeasibly large penis; Johnny Vegas is fat and unloved; Mark Gatiss falls in love with a dog; and Dominic Coleman can only find sexual satisfaction with strawberry jam and fish-paste sandwiches. *Viz*? Too subtle even for them.'

One of the kinder descriptions of the film was 'a sump of untreated dung'. 'Unspeakably vile' was another. Reviews from individual members of the public were more varied. These are here quoted verbatim.

Maybe I like the film because in my youth I knew guys like this, but regardless the film leaves nothing to the imagination. There are a number of real classic scenes including early on the woman with chronic dandruff serving chips with a coating of the same. Ok its not a great classic, but I do defy you to either not laugh or not recognise some of the characters as some guys you know (or ladies to that matter). Take it for what it is good boardy British Sex Humour and you won't be disappointed.

This film is one of the funniest films i have seen in a long time johnny vegas is golden and macenzie crook is even better when i read in the papers about this film all it got was bad reveiws but the humor is quick lots of one liners and a lot of familier faces that really shone in this the genre of the film which follows four potato delivery men in birmingham and there quest for sex is hilerious better than all the hype over films like the full monty this is a guaranteed crack up you'll love it!!!!!!!!!!!!

Which only goes to show how wrong the critics can be. Or right.

Quite what Messrs Gatiss, Vegas and Crook are doing in this dross in anyone's guess. Although I would have to suspect that a few quid for a couple of days' work had everything to do with it. This is a repellent piece of film making that features a witless script, flat direction, hopeless incidental music and a level of acting that could best be described as gurning.

Hmm, well, we can wish that some reviewers would get to the point and stop beating about the bush. Borrowing from the British film dark ages of smutty comedies such as *Confessions of a Window Cleaner*, even theoretically this film has the potential to be truly awful. And it really, really is. The childish innuendos hark back to the days when Britain was an embarrassingly sexually repressed nation. The script is what you'd expect a couple of 15-year-olds to knock up in a day. A horrendously bad film.

Possibly there might be a clue in the relative literacy of the good and bad reviews. After all, some people thought *Men in Black* was funny.

Adrian only just squeezes onto the cast list as 'host of a sex party', and none of the pukka reviews, good or bad, mention him. Still, there was one person at least who appreciated him, although coming to the film some years after its release in February 2004.

The best bit in this film is when Adrian 'One Show' Chiles answers the door at that sex party. I reckon

he's onto the fact that people are recognising him
for this scene and that's why he's let his bumfluff
grow recently? as a disguise!

Adrian's own memories of the film are typical of him: 'It
was harrowing because I was very overweight at the time.
I didn't realise until I saw myself semi-naked on screen. I
had a towel round my waist and looked like Joe Bugner
in his declining years. I tried to hitch the towel up to cover
my spare tyre, but the French continuity woman – who
was unspeakably beautiful – kept pulling it down.
Humiliating.'

There was also plenty of variety in his radio work. In July
2005, he did *In the Footsteps of Brad Pitt*, an explanation
of the work of a group of people called Foley artists. Named
after a great film sound-effects man, Jack Foley, these
inventive folk have what must be one of the most enjoyable
jobs in the world. They watch newly shot film, most of
which will have poor or nonexistent accompanying sound,
and create – or recreate – the right noises. So, Brad Pitt
might be filmed walking barefoot across a bathroom floor;
the Foley artists will record themselves actually walking
across a similar floor in time, or will fiddle it some other
way. When Mary Queen of Scots has her head chopped off,
they do it with a crisp cabbage.

According to one review, Adrian was 'a warm and
hilariously inept guide to this strange world'. One of his
jobs was the classic of trying to mimic, with two coconut
halves, the sound of a galloping horse. 'Sounds like a
drunk horse,' one Foley artist said. 'Speed it up a bit.
Right, now that's got seven legs.'

At 15 stone and with size 11 feet, Adrian then had to

be Keira Knightley. In heels, he said, 'Shut your eyes. Imagine this is Keira Knightley.' He and they failed, as he galumphed across the floor like, well, like a 15-stone bloke, or maybe a two-legged horse.

In early 2006, in a series of three programmes, Adrian explored the fates of the redundant workers from the Rover Longbridge plant, ex-Austin, ex-BMC, ex-British Leyland, and by then just ex. When he'd first arrived, at Q Gate at Longbridge in April 2005, only days after the closure had been announced, it was hardly surprising that many workers refused to be interviewed. Over the months, the team went back and back, and gradually won people's trust.

Adrian began the first programme with his shock at seeing the desolation. 'It's like something out of a children's story, where one day the factory stopped working. The heart's been cut out of their community. Six thousand have lost their jobs, probably the only job they've ever had since leaving school. Then, to top it off, Radio 4 tips up every few months to find out how it's all going. I'm sure that's just what the ex-MG Rover workers wanted.'

Going through the history of Longbridge gave the programme the context necessary to put it in the centre of the local community. 'It was like having an extended family, and not having it there now is like a bereavement.

'It was like the sudden death of a family member. I just couldn't believe it.'

Adrian was his sensitive, empathetic self but, no matter how sad most of it was, when one 57-year-old, who had lost his job after 32 years, turned out to be called Maurice Minor, there had to be a laugh in it somewhere.

A year later he went back again for two more programmes – and it wasn't just about jobs. Families, health, all sorts of issues were covered, and sympathetically. He, being a Brummie, felt for them more than many would have.

Professional storytelling made another fascinating subject in January 2007, an ancient art practised by those imaginative and compelling people who were making their own 'programmes' before ever there was radio or television or cinema, and who now are enjoying something of a revival.

What I'd Really Like To Do was a television series following 10 trades or professions, voted by the viewing public as their perfect jobs. Starting with zookeeper at tenth most popular, Adrian went up the scale. For actor, Adrian had Georgina Bouzova as his subject, who had jacked in her lawyer's career and was now happy as nurse Ellen Zitec in *Casualty* (and had appeared in *Strictly Come Dancing* Series 4). Here's what one viewer thought:

For us idle gits who can watch daytime TV the BBC are running a series in which Adrian Chiles tries out the top ten desirable jobs as selected by an opinion poll. The fourth most desired job is that of a pilot and this programme is to be shown on Monday, January 8 at 9:15 am (BBC1). Based on his amusing attempts to reveal the reality of some of the other jobs, it should be quite good. Interestingly, being a pilot is considered much more desirable than being a footballer or doctor, but slightly less desirable than being an archaeologist or a fashion photographer.

Had Adrian asked Christine, she might well have said, 'I'd like to fly helicopters. Air ambulance or air-sea rescue or something like that. And in my spare time, ironing. I know it's boring but I'm madly obsessed with ironing.'

Adrian left *Working Lunch* in January 2007, as *The One Show* was beginning to take over as his major interest. His co-presenter Adam Shaw stayed on for another 18 months before he too packed it in. Viewers' comments were predictable.

Bring back the old Working Lunch format and its team. The new style looks more like a game show. No wonder the viewing figures have dipped. The BBC can't see a winner when they have one. Put the old show back together with its straightforward, no-gimmicks presentation – the best daytime TV.

I used to watch this avidly with the old presenters, but when they changed the format – for no reason at all, it was a very successful show as it was – I found it missable.

People who like to tinker with success are frequent, you'd think they would learn from the Coke New Formula story – put it back to how it was!

Working Lunch is another example of the BBC trying to fix something that wasn't broken in the first place. Working Lunch nowadays is? dire and similar to every other business program. Bring back the old presenters and the quirky reporting style.

In February 2007, newspapers reported that BBC presenter Adrian Chiles was among a number of the corporation's stars to have been sent soiled toilet paper in the post. *Match of the Day 2* host Chiles said he had received about eight packages, which he described as 'disgusting. The smell of someone else's shit is not something you want first thing in the morning,' he said.

According to the *Sun*, 'police are investigating a string of packages posted to some of broadcasting's best-known names since mid-January'. In a statement, the BBC refused to disclose the names of the other corporation staff who had also received the unwanted mail in recent weeks, nor would it confirm that other presenters had been targeted, adding it did not like to comment on individual cases.

'From time to time, BBC presenters and staff do receive malicious and nuisance mail, although we do try to intercept it wherever possible. We try to avoid commenting on individual cases because, very often, those sending such mail gain pleasure from publicity. When we can identify the sender of such materials, they can expect a visit from the police.'

CHAPTER SEVEN

THE DREAM TEAM— 2008 AND ON

The year began with proof, as if Christine ever doubted it, of the madness of the world when she was invited to attend a celebrity Burns Night, at Harvey Nichols, with her *One Show* colleague Hardeep Singh Kohli. He went in kilt and turban. To their credit, they ran the gauntlet of paparazzi fairly swiftly, unlike some of the B-list actresses who clearly thought it was the Oscars.

It was an Olympic year. Adrian was asked for his comments on being appointed as part of the BBC team: 'For me, I think the Olympics represents the apotheosis of all the usual stuff about sport: the dedication, the glory, the disappointment, the tension, the joy, the despair . . . But it's also the chance to learn about different sports and become passionate about them in a very short space of time. Also, brilliant though they are, the competitors often are purely athletes, not celebrities. And that makes it so much more special.

'My favourite Olympic memories are the stuff I saw as

a kid: Ovett, Coe, Thompson, Foster etc. It was so magical. Also the moments of sheer drama: I remember Olga Korbut falling off the beam and crying. I was absolutely captivated. I remember my dad saying she'd be sent to Siberia as a punishment and I didn't know whether he was joking.

'I really can't wait for Beijing. I just have no preconceptions, which is fascinating. I've been to Hong Kong and Macau but doubt that's much preparation for Beijing. Once there, I'm really looking forward to seeing the cycling, table tennis, badminton, athletics and weightlifting. As far as British hopes go, Tom Daley seems to have some pretty unstoppable momentum.

'Looking ahead to 2012, assuming it's a massive success, which I think it will be, London, and the UK as a whole, will have a newfound sense of itself. I sense all athletes work as hard as they possibly can, but the added incentive of competing on home soil will surely give them a little extra.'

Olympic Breakfast, 6.00–9.00am BBC One/BBC HD: Hazel Irvine and Adrian Chiles start the day with a look at the main news from the day's events and some live coverage from the early afternoon's action in Beijing, also incorporating national and regional news and weather.

Here's one view of it:

You sit up all night with Rishi Persad, and what's your reward? Adrian bloody Chiles. That's what the license fee is being used on, flying him to

Beijing? As if that's not bad enough, he's forgotten the delightful Christine Bleakley from *The One Show*, so we get Hazel Irvine and her massive teeth.

Olympics 2008, 9.00am–noon BBC One/BBC HD: Hazel Irvine and Adrian Chiles present live coverage of the rowing, sailing and cycling.

Adrian had never been to an Olympics before. He said it was a good job they come around only every four years because he would need that long to get over this one. He was deeply impressed by the pressures of the work and the quality of his fellow presenters.

'We have to be almost as quick as the athletes. All I'd done before in international sport was football. In Germany we had 64 matches in 32 days. In Beijing, 302 events in 16 days. Getting your head around all those rules and competitors is impossible. Unless you're Hazel Irvine.'

On his first day, he went to do an interview about Daisy Dick, believing that to be the name of a dressage horse. He found out seconds before the interview that Daisy was the rider. Admiration grew and grew for the dedication of the competitors, who had trained for years and could be out of the Games in a few moments; but there were comic memories too, such as being stuck in a taxi with Sharron Davies because their driver couldn't read the name of their hotel.

When the men's 100-metres final was due to be run, Adrian wasn't commentating and so was free, if he wanted, to watch West Brom and Arsenal on the TV. A colleague advised the 100-metres final, offering a rare and privileged experience, whereas he could watch West Brom getting stuffed any day of the week.

At the table tennis, there was high excitement as his old pal Zoran Primorac, Croatian player from Adrian's early days on the *Birmingham Post*, reached the last 16 with a breathtaking rally, then got to the quarterfinals, where he lost to Jörgen Persson.

Television is something of a competitive sport, too. On one competitive evening in mid-June 2008, a televised Coldplay concert delivered 1.1 million viewers and a 6 per cent share to BBC2 in the 45 minutes from 7pm. *Channel 4 News* from 7pm had 1 million viewers, while Channel Five's 7pm news had 316,000. Thus we can see that the Coldplay concert was less popular than BBC1's *The One Show*, presented by Adrian and Christine, with 4.1 million viewers and a 22 per cent share from 7pm. *Emmerdale* won the slot with 6 million viewers and a 31 per cent share for ITV1 at the same time.

These figures show just how well known our two from-nowheres were becoming. As well as chipping away at *Emmerdale*, attracting viewers, Adrian was already attracting offers from ITV. He said, 'What ITV offered was very well paid, just doing a few dozen football matches a year. I suppose that if I hadn't had this, I would have gone. But you can't beat a show like this. They come along once in a lifetime.'

And, after a year or so on *The One Show*, Christine was sufficiently in the public eye to be invited to compete in *Strictly Come Dancing*, and to be linked with other television stations. When Fiona Phillips, regarded by many as the best thing about *GMTV*, announced her departure, all sorts of rumours flashed around the media's chatterers. Who could be similarly bubbly, similarly sharp, and who would appeal to an audience seen to be families, yes, but mainly the mums? The job was worth £400,000 a year, rather more than Christine was on, so whether it would be she, or Kate Silverton of BBC News, or Ulrika Jonsson kept the tongues a-wagging in many London restaurants and bars. One source said that journalists might as well add Dot Cotton, Angelina Jolie and Lassie, because they'd be just as near the mark.

Far more important, as it turned out, was *Strictly*. Christine's professional partner was nominated as Matthew Cutler, the 2007 winner with Alesha Dixon. The list of competitors was leaked, naturally, and Sky Bet was first into the market with the odds.

Favourite at 4/1, *Holby City* actor Tom Chambers. Mark Foster, international swimmer, 7/1. Glamour girls Christine Bleakley, Lisa Snowdon, Jodie Kidd, Rachel Stevens, Jessie Wallace, all at 9/1.

Tennis player and *GMTV* presenter Andrew Castle, 10/1. Slightly older glamour girls Heather Small and Cherie Lunghi, 11/1. Rugby international Austin Healey, 12/1.

Madcap chef Gary Rhodes, *EastEnders/Footballers' Wives* sex bomb Gillian Taylforth, both 16/1. Actor and *EastEnders*' Phil Daniels, 20/1. Political journalist and guru John Sergeant, and *Rising Damp* star Don Warrington, rank outsiders at 25/1.

For a joint third favourite, Christine surely was not exactly boiling over with confidence. 'It's hard when we're training because I feel I'm not good enough. I look at Matthew and he's so brilliant, gliding around the floor without any effort at all, and I think, "Look, I'm supposed to be concentrating on what's going on here. I'm very lucky to have him." He's gorgeous, and wonderful.

'But, big but, nobody could be better than Alesha. She was utterly superb, so the first thing I had to do when I met Matthew was apologise. Sorry, but you can't expect two wins in a row.

'I'm a hard worker, but I'm not competitive in that sense, not like I imagine Austin Healey is, or Mark Foster. I mean, international sports stars, they must have that in them. The producers want me to be competitive, like it's *MasterChef* or something, but it's not in my nature. And, the other thing: I've never danced before. I'm not from that background, you know, stage school, ballet classes, so I'm starting from nothing but the Belfast version of *Saturday Night Fever*. I'm a beginner.'

Christine's first dance would be the foxtrot. 'It's feet, it's legs, it's head and neck, it's your whole body. If it doesn't come naturally, as it doesn't with me, all these little things have to be thought about and remembered, meanwhile performing for the judges and the viewers. So that's another disadvantage. I'm on telly, but I've never been on a stage as The Act. Look at the other girls. Gillian Taylforth, actress. Jessie Wallace, actress. Heather, singer, Cherie, actress, Jodie, model, Lisa, model, Rachel, singer. They're all used to it, being up there in front of crowds of real people. I'll just have to forget about my mum thinking I'm showing off again, and get on with it.'

Christine's feelings of being an amateur among professionals came to the fore again when the girls went for a fitting. 'I felt self-conscious next to Lisa Snowdon and Jodie Kidd. They're experienced models. They don't think anything of getting their kit off in front of people.

You can't afford that sort of modesty when you're changing for the catwalk. But I'm not used to it. I hid behind the dresser person. If there had been beach towels there I'd have wrapped myself in them.'

When the question of shortness of skirt came up, the girls who worked on the costumes wanted Christine to go shorter. She was not so sure. She didn't want to be overtly or aggressively sexy, and she didn't want to be in a beauty competition with Lisa and the others, who, she felt, looked fabulous without having to dance a step. Anyone pooh-poohing her lack of confidence, telling her she could more than hold her own in any such company, got a firm response.

'You should see me next to them. They're the stunners. I'm used to Belfast, where everyone knows everyone. I mean, I still get excited about going shopping in Oxford Street. They're the big city sophisticates. I'm the schoolgirl on the end.'

Nerves were more settled when the actual competition started. It was the men in the first show. Next week, it was the girls. Here's Christine: 'Tomorrow night I'm going to be performing my first solo dance on *Strictly Come Dancing*. It's a foxtrot and I've been rehearsing as much as possible to get it right, which has been hard seeing as I also have a full-time job on *The One Show*.

'I'm really excited that the time has now arrived for me to perform. John Sergeant did really well last week and I just hope I can keep up the standard he has set. I just want to get on with it now. Matthew and I have such a laugh together so I'm just going to try and enjoy it, but it has been a week of butterflies. I'll be gutted if I go on Saturday, I'll cry, although I half expect it.'

What, Christine? You cannot be serious.

'Anyway, I really appreciate all your messages of support and best wishes on the website, thanks very much. Wish me luck.'

And so they did, with plenty of exclamation marks.

Go for it Christine – you sparkle like a diamond on *The One Show* (alongside that cheeky monkey Chiles!) and I'm sure you'll sparkle like a star on the Strictly dancefloor!

Matt is the best pro so I really wanted him to have another really good celebrity partner this year, and you stood out to me as the best of the female line-up. However, when I watched the preview show last Saturday, I was a little disappointed as you seemed so negative, worrying about showing a bit of leg, calling yourself gangly. Well, listen to me young lady! You are one of the best looking female celebrities appearing this year (you and Rachel Stevens are the most striking!). You are young and fit. You are taking part in one of the best-loved TV programmes – what a wonderful opportunity! So make the absolute MOST of this. You don't want to look back and have any regrets, do you? You have the ABSOLUTE BEST professional partner – Matt is brilliant at both Latin and Ballroom and he is the MOST patient so you are in the best of hands! So PLEASE just enjoy the whole experience. Come out on that dance floor and dance your heart out. Put on the act the audience wants to see. Make us believe in the dances. And DON'T compare yourself to Alesha. Be you. You and Matt will be great together. I'm really hoping that you'll be in that Final and, who knows...even win the competition! You can do it! Oh...and I hope you'll be taking time off from the *One Show* later on in order to practice more. You won't be able to do both. Give this all you've got. Go girl!!

I think you have a fantastic figure and I'll vote for you anyday regardless of whether you can dance or not. Just walk out, show a bit of leg, and you've got my vote!

'Christine is gorgeous and hopefully wins the show' – by Neil. 'Christine rocks!!' – by Millie. 'We just love Christine Bleakley. The most genuine celeb on Strictly!' – by Sarah. 'I Think she is the most sexy women on TV hope she do well' – by Keith. 'i think she is well rubbish' – by sophie. 'Christine Bleakley is lovely and I hope she wins' – by paul.

OK, everyone. Here we go. Christine is with Matthew Cutler. She's worried her dad will think her skirts are too short, and feels intimidated by the skills last year of the brilliant Alesha, and this year by Lisa and Jodie, who are natural performers (as opposed to ex-floor managers, presumably).

Christine and Matthew's dance is a foxtrot, to 'The Way You Look Tonight', which must be one of the loveliest tunes ever written (by Jerome Kern), originally for Fred Astaire to sing to Ginger Rogers. How can we not join in? Someday, when I'm awfully low, when the world is cold, I will feel a glow just thinking of you, and the way you look tonight.

Christine looks wonderful tonight in a sparkly pink dress but she struggles with your actual dancing. Her expression has a frozen dimension, the one so often described as 'rabbit in the headlights' by journalists who have never seen a rabbit in the headlights. Matt appears to be singing the words. You're lovely, with your smile so warm, and your cheeks so soft, there is nothing for me but to love you, and the way you look tonight.

To the judges. Big boss Len says it was beautiful. Bruno says ethereal. Craig says well controlled. Arlene says coltish Christine, and there is some sort of an argument about the problem being Christine's body, as if maybe she was built for something else.

Christine says that Matthew is brilliant. Craig gives her 6, Arlene 6, Len a very generous 8, Bruno 7. Len gets himself in bother with his scoring. He gives someone 8, then he sees someone better who has therefore to be given 9, and he runs out of scores. But it was Gillian Taylforth who was, as the late rugby commentator Eddie Waring might have put it, for the early bath – or, more correctly, for the tears and brave smiles in the bar afterwards.

Despite all the hoo-ha about John Sergeant and the slewing of votes his way, Christine kept going. The next time, she and Matthew did a very smart and professional dance and got nines.

This is what one viewer thought of her double-Latin night:

I'm slightly in love with Christine and I think the public is too. She's very pretty and has a lovely way about her, and I'm convinced that her personality is helping her to stay in the competition. She's a good dancer but not as sharp as the others. This lack of sharpness really showed last night. Despite getting acting lessons from Felicity Kendall in training, her tango was a bit leaden and limp – none of the passion and aggression the dance requires, none of the stampy moves I enjoy in the tango. Again the music was rubbish. Why did they do it to Robert Palmer's Addicted To Love? They should really keep it Argentinian. Craig said it was simply not good enough for this stage of the competition. Craig 6, Arlene 7, Len 8, Bruno 7.

Her next dance, the salsa, was better but the standard the others were setting was beginning to look ominous. Craig 7, Arlene 7, Len 8, Bruno 8.

Now for the cha-cha. It is obligatory in Latin American for the lady to wear almost nothing and, after the – also obligatory – non-dancing bit of film with schoolkids, Christine took the floor in a red dress, which, being in shreds, could only have been worn by a Christine. She looked utterly fabulous but the judges had eyes only for the mechanics of the thing.

Wooden, not enough sexy hips, feel the song more. Arlene even showed what she means with the hips. Sit down, Arlene, you ain't a Christine no more. Len said Arlene was talking piffle, although he agreed Christine needed a harder sell. She should 'whip off her knickers and fling them in the air'.

Craig 6, Arlene 6, sexy Len 8, Bruno 7, which made 27. Not enough, maybe. First time in the bottom two.

Thankfully, viewers disagreed and she was through to the next shoot-out.

We all know what happened next. Having managed to avoid the dance-off all series, Christine found herself in the bottom two again, with Rachel Stevens. Christine and Matthew Cutler tangoed; Rachel and Vincent Simone waltzed. The four judges agreed it was the end for Christine.

Craig Revel Horwood said, 'Both couples danced their hearts out tonight. That was obvious, but the couple I am going to save for the quarterfinals are Rachel and Vincent.'

Christine, typically self-deprecating, could hardly believe she'd got so far, anyway. 'I thought I would go in the first week. That I didn't is entirely down to Matthew. He's been incredible. And I can't thank people enough for their support, all over the country, not just Northern Ireland. I think I'm going to miss seeing Matthew every day more than anything else.'

Nothing became her so much as her leaving. In doing so, she was seen by more people than watched any other show. That results programme of *Strictly Come Dancing*, which saw Christine Bleakley depart, attracted 9.7 million viewers and a 34 per cent audience share between 8.15pm and 9pm, which was the biggest for any show on the night. A year later, rumours went around that Christine would replace Tess Daly as the new hostess of the show.

Sorry, Christine, but my biggest laugh so far on *The One Show* was the clip of you on *Strictly Come Dancing*. Never mind, just think of the royalties

every time it is put on air. I think you blushed with
great dignity. Keep it up everyone in front and
behind the camera, it's a great programme.

In that same dancing year, 2008, MPG – which can stand
for Media Planning Group as well as miles per gallon and
Maine Potato Growers, and which has as its mission 'the
establishment of relevant contact points between brands
and consumers in order to deliver results' – gave Adrian
Chiles a total television audience of 1.04 billion.

By the simple expedient of adding together the audience
figures given for every one of his shows from 1 January to
18 December 2008, MPG concluded that he was Britain's
most watched. When not fronting *The One Show*, he also
presented *Match of the Day 2* in a more informal way than
the original, and had his fun with *The Apprentice: You're
Fired!*, an amusing postmortem with those at whom my
lord of Sugar had pointed his finger; also, he'd garnered a
large audience with his morning broadcasts from the
Beijing Olympics, all adding up to a notional total of over
a billion viewers, more than Ant and Dec – and there are
two of them. In typical Chiles fashion, this news was
received with, 'If I'm the most watched person, all I can
say is there can't be much on television.'

What there was on telly, in fact, was this: 239 episodes
of *The One Show*, with an average audience of 3.6
million, to give an aggregate of more than 860 million; 33
of *MOTD2*, with an average audience of 2.39 million,
giving an aggregate of 79 million; 12 of *The Apprentice:
You're Fired!*, average audience 4.58 million, aggregate
55 million. Plus, an estimated 46 million watched him
present his share of the BBC's Olympics coverage.

It is perhaps illuminating, or perhaps not, to see whom the honest, sonsie-faced one beat in this competition he didn't know he'd entered. At number two was Phillip Schofield with *This Morning*, *Mr and Mrs* and *Dancing on Ice*, in round figures 678 million. Three was Noel Edmonds and *Deal or No Deal*, 612 million. Four, Fern Britton with *This Morning* and *Mr and Mrs*, 494 million. We must ask if the people who watched *Mr and Mrs* were counted twice, or cut in half, to appear on the totals of Phil and Fern. Could be vitally important.

At five we had the lovely Davina McCall and *Big Brother*, 404 million, and at six Dermot O'Leary with *The X Factor*, 359 million. (Why pick on him? What about Simon and Cheryl?) Number seven was Ant & Dec with *I'm a Celebrity* and *Britain's Got Talent*, 315 million. Now, just a minute you MPG fellows. Shouldn't that be equal seventh for Ant and Dec as separate presenting persons, if you follow the Phil-and-Fern rule? Or, it should be Ant with 157.5 million and Dec with 157.5 million, assuming that both are watched with equal enthusiasm.

Eighth, or ninth if Ant and Dec were equal seventh, was Gary Lineker with *Match of the Day* and *Ryder Cup highlights*, 302 million. Next was Holly Willoughby with *The Xtra Factor*, *Celebrity Juice* and *Dancing on Ice* (see Schofield above, this gets more and more complicated), 250 million. Tenth, or eleventh, was Paul O'Grady and *The Paul O'Grady Show*, 245 million.

Well done, everyone.

Millions more – well, maybe hundreds, or just close family – were also expected to be listening to Adrian on a Christmas record, released in early December 2008 in plenty of time for a surge to the number-one spot. A report stated that the 'dancing pig in Cuban heels' – John Sergeant – who won the hearts of the nation on *Strictly Come Dancing*, had announced plans to release a Christmas single. 'Let's Not Fight This Christmas' was written by Squeeze's Chris Difford to be a collaboration between Sergeant and Adrian Chiles and Christine Bleakley of *The One Show*.

In the struggle for pop supremacy, Sergeant was said to have one distinct advantage: he couldn't sing. This report seriously underplayed the Bleakley-Chiles contribution, in fact, the contribution of the whole *One Show* team. It was really their record with added Sergeant, and if you ever saw the film of it you would see that the latter was not the only one who couldn't sing, or dance for that matter.

Adrian looked decidedly uncomfortable in what you might have called the pop video, if you hadn't seen it and were feeling generous, whereas the lovely Christine was dancing elegance personified, in a very understated way. This was not Master Difford's finest hour as a composer, either, but the whole thing swung along gamely. Alas, some nobody who just happened to have won *The X Factor* topped the charts and *The One Show* single never even crept into the top 100.

Still, as a piece of comedy, it is not possible to commend the dancing rehearsals highly enough. Adrian clearly cannot tell his left from his right nor his boogie from his woogie, and his claim that John Sergeant put him off the correct steps is right up there with Baron Münchausen's biggest porkies.

By 2009, everyone in the BBC, even the most senior

executives, had realised that the boy from Brum and the sweet colleen from somewhere or other (Scotland, was it? no, Ireland I think; Ireland? really? good heavens!), had pushed *The One Show* into heights undreamed of when it started.

The pair of solo presenters had become a double act, celebrated enough in their own right to present BAFTA awards, but also seen as individual talents to be cherished by the BBC. Adrian did a competent job with the rebellious panellists on *Have I Got News for You*. Christine, for example, was said to have been offered Fern Britton's spot on *This Morning* as well as Fiona Phillips's job on *GMTV*.

'I think there have been calls,' said Christine, 'but I haven't even talked to my agent about it. Manoeuvres behind closed doors. Smoke-filled rooms, all that, before you hear anything. Anyway, who wants to get up that early in the morning? I have enough trouble getting into *The One Show* studio at lunchtime. I'm happy where I am.' So happy, it was said, that she turned down a firm offer and took a pay cut to stay with Adrian on *The One Show*.

Many people would have liked her on *This Morning*, or *GMTV*, but not all.

Methinks Ms Bleakley's publicity machine has got above itself. She's far too lightweight, immensely irritating and whilst attractive it ends as soon as she opens her mouth and speaks like she has a mouthful of nails.

Oh, dear! There's always one. Meanwhile, the real Christine had apparently had arguments with boyfriend

Mark Beirne during the Christmas holidays, basically about work versus relationship, not an unfamiliar story, before travelling to Uganda in early January with Comic Relief. This, she said, made her re-evaluate her life – another not unfamiliar story.

'I came across this wee girl called Hajara, who is sixteen, and whose mum died of AIDS three years ago, leaving Hajara to look after her brothers and sisters when her father went off with another woman. That day changed how I see everything. It sounds so ridiculous and such a cliché, but it really did. It puts everything in your life in perspective when you see something like that. You come back to our civilisation, and you can just hop in a shower and turn the hot water on and you've got clean clothes and you can buy a pint of milk. Hajara can't do any of those things, but she still gets on with life and hope.

'I have to admit that at first I wanted to get out of going to Uganda. I thought I was going to find it really tough and I just wanted to be at home. But I'm so relieved I went because it's the best thing I've ever done. I've always watched Comic Relief but nothing could have prepared me for this. The stench of raw sewage was overpowering. You had to take time to adjust to be able to breathe. There was no hope in the eyes of the children. The eyes of Hajara and her brothers and sisters were empty. I got very upset and had to take a break. She smiled at me and rubbed my arm, and told me it was OK. I felt guilty because she shouldn't have been comforting me, seeing me crying like a complete wimp.

'I drove away feeling drained. The whole day had been horrifying. But in the middle of this horror is so much goodness, including the help of the organisations funded by Comic Relief. These people don't want charity. They want to work and be independent. A small loan or a grant to a co-operative can work wonders.'

Only a week or so went by before the nation was informed that Christine and Mark had finally split. Mark was quoted as saying that they'd had too much time apart. Some of the papers said Mark had dumped her. Some said the other way around. Christine's associates said no one else was involved. Mark's friends blamed it on Adrian.

Christine explained that she had tried to get home as often as possible, but that seemingly wasn't often enough. The house they shared in south Belfast was put on the market, as was Mark's Belfast bar, the House Pub & Kitchen, in the student quarter on Stranmillis Road, only a hundred yards from Christine's old stamping ground at Queen's. The pub offered 'everything you could want from a local pub including an extensive mouth-watering cocktail list and delicious lunch and dinner menus. In good weather customers can laze in the beer garden equipped with its very own outside bar. Students can take advantage of the Curry Club (Curry and a drink of your choice for just £5.50) or The Meal for Two Deal (two main courses and a bottle of wine for just £24.95).'

No curry club in my day, Christine might have said, as she finally decided that London and work and Mark could not all go together. She was also growing up fast in the new media world she now inhabited. Media attention? 'That's par for the course. When you work in TV you expect it and you deal with it.' Even so, she cancelled a round of Belfast interviews that had been scheduled for her to promote Comic Relief events.

Since being given *The One Show* permanently, Christine had been staying in her London flat during the week and flying back to Belfast at weekends. As she said, such a relationship cannot go on for ever. Then came *Strictly*, with its daily rehearsals on top of *The One Show* five nights a week, plus the live show on Saturday nights.

Now it was Mark doing the flying, to join the *Strictly* audience to support Christine. Friends asked him why, when Christine was dancing, the camera always cut away to Adrian and not to him.

At least the next bit of media fluttering had nothing to do with Christine. Views were divided over a row that blew up when a *One Show* regular, Carol Thatcher, used a word she shouldn't have. Reactions ranged from 'sack the racist cow, she only got the job because of her mother anyway', to 'the words storm and teacup spring to mind', when Ms Thatcher slipped up in the post-show green room. She was talking tennis and the Australian Open, saying that one of the frogs might win: 'You know, that froggy golliwog guy.' The comedian Jo Brand, who had been on the show, didn't think much of that and neither did Adrian, and neither did the powers that be, who terminated the Thatcher connection with the show. The BBC had well over 2,000 complaints against the sacking, and 60 or so in support.

Adrian had been here before. Back in 2004 he had written the documentary *What Ron Said*, in which Ron Atkinson, famous football manager, tried to find out why one unguarded moment and one offensive word finished his career as a TV pundit. Soon, *The One Show* was there again too, when resident reporter Hardeep Singh Kohli was suspended from duty for six months after he admitted, and apologised for, 'inappropriate behaviour' with a female researcher. It is perhaps mildly interesting to reflect that 30 or even 20 years ago none of these incidents would have been considered worth mentioning, much less been sufficiently important to be career threatening.

Guinness World Records (formerly *The Guinness Book of Records*) holds a strange attraction, and it's always news. So nothing could be better than Adrian making an attempt on the world record for the number of kisses received in one minute. The definition of a kiss states that it cannot be an air kiss, that there must be contact from the kissers' lips, but no particular parts of the kissee's person are specified.

The live attempt on *The One Show* went ahead after military-style planning, although the military in question was probably the Ruritanian navy. Adrian faced front with two lines of volunteers behind him. As the lines of kissers moved forwards, he swayed like a windscreen wiper to receive kisses from left and right in turn. He could not see if they were male or female, although if they were all female he complained that there were some very bristly ones.

When the minute was up, the official timekeeper announced that 78 kisses had been planted. This was claimed as a record, although it fell some way short of other claims. We have to put it down as a possible and no more than that.

Here's a couple of official announcements. The BBC put out a press release about *The One Show*, that little half-hour magazine on in the early weekday evenings, not requiring anything like the organisation and support that *GMTV* needed for its many hours a week, and yet somehow managing to attract something like five times the viewers.

Date: 03.08.2009

Category: BBC One; TV Entertainment; Factual & Arts TV

BBC One today announces that *The One Show* is set to be extended. Plus top names to provide holiday cover over summer – Gloria Hunniford, Gethin Jones, John Sergeant and Myleene Klass are welcomed as stand-in presenters.

After successfully trialling a 60-minute format of the show in May, the series, which usually runs at 30 minutes, will include an hour-long show every week from September to the end of the year.

The 60-minute shows will include a raft of new features, celebrating lives, landscapes and stories from all around the UK.

BBC One also announces today that *The One Show*'s presenters, Christine Bleakley and Adrian Chiles, will be taking a well-deserved fortnight's holiday in August.

The channel is delighted to be welcoming some of the country's most popular presenters to stand in during their absence.

Gloria Hunniford and Gethin Jones take the helm from Monday 17 to Friday 21 August.

They will be followed by everyone's favourite dancer John Sergeant who will join forces with Myleene Klass, from Monday 24 to Friday 28 August.

Executive Producer of *The One Show*, Tessa Finch, says: 'We're delighted to welcome four *One Show* favourites to stand in for Christine and Adrian while they're on holiday.'

The hour-long shows will start in September 2009 and the specific day is to be confirmed.

Notes to Editors

The One Show was two years old on 9 July 2009.

Average audience viewing figures (year to date) for *The One Show*: 4.4 million.

A number of high-profile guests have appeared on the programme, including: Kate Winslet, Sir Michael Caine, Morrissey, Stephen Fry, Bette Midler, Jeremy Clarkson, David Duchovny, Dame Helen Mirren, Liam Neeson, Tom Jones, Lionel Richie, Lily Allen, James Nesbitt, Joanna Lumley, Ricky Gervais, Annie Lennox, Patrick Stewart, Mr T, Julie Walters, Sir Michael Parkinson, Fern Britton, Vic and Bob, French and Saunders, Michael McIntyre, Nigella Lawson and Adam Sandler.

No mention there of the slalom mobility scooter race between Meatloaf and Adrian, which Christine had to pronounce a draw because of cheating by both drivers.

ADRIAN CHILES AND CHRISTINE BLEAKLEY

Date: 01.09.2009

Category: BBC One; TV Entertainment; Factual &
Arts TV

The One Show: Monday 7 to Friday 11 September,
2009

7.00–7.30pm BBC ONE (Monday–Thursday)
7.00–8.00pm BBC ONE (Friday)

The One Show kicks off a new series with some exciting autumn strands including, on Fridays, a new hour-long show. Following the successful trial of the 60-minute format in May, the series, which runs for 30 minutes from Monday to Thursday, includes this new, one-hour show every week from September until the end of the year.

The 60-minute shows will include new features celebrating lives, landscapes and stories from around the UK.

Combining celebrity guests with topical reports, *The One Show* has established itself as essential early-evening viewing. The autumn line-up is packed with its usual eclectic mix, including history, natural history, science, geology, astronomy, art, literature, music and architecture. There's also a new member of the team with Jay Rayner, best known as *The Observer*'s food critic, getting to grips with food-based consumer reports and shedding new light on the science of food. Jay joins the *One Show* presenters Adrian Chiles and Christine Bleakley.

Tessa Finch, *The One Show*'s executive producer, says:

'*The One Show* has had a great summer and is gearing up for autumn with a brilliant line-up of stories from all around the UK and some extremely exciting projects for viewers to get involved with. The new hour-long programmes are a great vote of confidence from the audience and the channel. Everyone on *The One Show* is looking forward to the challenge. We'll be remaining true to *The One Show*'s commitment to intelligent fun.

There you have it. Intelligent fun. And a new one-hour show on a Friday. Everything was going so well. Christine certainly was loving it. 'I love long lunches and lost afternoons. When you're live on the telly at 7pm five nights a week, they're a thing of the past, but it's well worth it. Dolly Parton, for instance, completely blew me away. She's an utter pro and a great interview and I couldn't believe she was right beside me. She held my hand while she was talking to me, which was unbelievable. The Eagles were a bit tricky, but American guests do come on and look a bit shocked. They don't know the show and they're like, "We've got to talk about butterflies?" So I just smile and say that's right. People who I've expected to be divas and prima donnas have been surprisingly gracious. Liza Minnelli, for instance. When I was a floor manager I saw a lot of divas. Maybe they're just nicer to me now I'm doing this job.

'Fan mail is email these days. We get 10,000 emails a night. That's ten. Thousand. Which is an incredible amount. A lot of them are about what I wear and what I look like, as if it really matters to people. It must do. They are trying to be helpful, to help me look my best. They say things like "Your hair was great last night, better than tonight. It suits you better that other way." I've had marriage proposals, too. One clearly expected the answer yes, inviting me on his yacht, you know, like Tony Curtis in *Gentlemen Prefer Blondes*. There was a timetable with pickup points, flight tickets, the lot. And no, I didn't go.'

Christine's interview with Dame Vera Lynne contained some good advice for the younger woman who, perhaps a little nervous with such a great personality in the armchair opposite, was cuddling a comfort cushion. Dame Vera described how she had found the type of song that suited her, with nice words and an easy tune that people could remember, and she'd stuck with that. 'If you find something that is right for you, stay with it. Don't be tempted to do something that is completely alien to you.'

Both *One Show* presenters felt restricted by 30 minutes. Christine called it 'the biggest problem we have. We can get into a serious conversation that's going somewhere, and you've got somebody on the floor shouting "two minutes". It's frustrating when we've asked the right questions but don't have time to get the right answer.'

Adrian, with his news-journalist roots, saw the difficulty rather more starkly. 'I miss haranguing people. I haven't harangued anyone in bloody years. That's what I was good at. I used to get someone on and haul him over the hot coals. Our show isn't like that. But we try not to let it get too soft. That was a concern before I got involved and it still is. Christine says there's a *One Show* way, which she thinks is the right way, and I think maybe there isn't always.'

Another problem, besides the balance between fun and serious, has always been the balance between studio and filmed items. It sometimes meant that a five-minute film wandering gently down a canal or meandering across meadows, left a tight schedule for a studio interview. This could annoy Adrian. Why should he have to rush and compress, when the film spent ages looking at a buttercup?

'Tessa, the producer, says that the research shows that our viewers like the film bits more than the studio bits, but that's not my experience,' said Christine. 'Our mail is full of questions about us and the guests. If Adrian's got a button undone, or I have, they notice. We are an integral part of the show, and not just the people filling in between the director saying "roll VTR". We're not just glue.'

The 60-minute Friday show at least gave them more time to talk to the guests. Christine's favourite sport was asking showbiz people difficult questions about bats and badgers, or whatever. Or bikinis.

'The *Mail on Sunday* thought the great British people would be interested in seeing shots of me in a bikini. That a newspaper should think it had such a great scoop, well, that takes some getting your head around. Of course, it's a shock the first time something like that happens. You don't imagine it, but you get used to it.'

What about seeing yourself on TV? Is that different from seeing your picture in a newspaper? Adrian wouldn't know because he never watches TV. 'I haven't seen myself on telly for years. That's not because I'm arrogant. It's because I can't bear it. Sometimes she'll make me watch something back on iPlayer so that I can see myself being a twat.'

So who was the boss? It looked like Adrian may have been, with Christine's permission. 'I check my jokes and everything with her first.' And what about the ITV offer?

'Great people, Michael Grade and Peter Fincham. It was sorely tempting. The same money for just doing football twice a week. But I liked it better here. With her.'

Christine felt the same. 'Look. The managers and the researchers study the figures. We just know whether something's right. And *The One Show* is right, and right for us. And no matter what the papers say about Simon Cowell and *The X Factor*, I know nothing about it.'

As well as *The One Show*, Christine was still doing TV for BBC1 Northern Ireland, for example *Christine Bleakley's Dancehall Sweethearts*, a nostalgic series following the romantic personal stories of couples who danced and romanced in Northern Ireland's favourite dancehalls during the 1940s, 1950s and 1960s.

Links with the province remained close. She was still a patron of the CineMagic Festival, a major effort in Northern Ireland to get children and young adults involved in all aspects of film-making. Her fellow patrons include Julian Fellowes, Brian Cox, Dermot O'Leary and many other luminaries willing to give their time to the future of their industry.

Another charity interest of Christine's is the Prince's Trust in Northern Ireland, where she acts as a Trust ambassador. Around one in five young people in Northern Ireland is not in work, education or training. In a given year, Prince's Trust Northern Ireland will support 3,000 young people to get their lives working. They give practical and financial support to the young people who need it most, helping to develop key skills, confidence and motivation, and enabling young people to move into work, education or training.

Save the Children is a magnet for TV people, partly because they are in such a good position to appeal to people's generosity, and because they're so good at it. Here's a joint appeal from Adrian and Christine:

Almost 10 million children under the age of 5 die every year. That's a coach load of children every 3 minutes. The majority of these deaths are preventable. A £5 mosquito net will stop a child catching malaria. We're supporting Save the Children's campaign to save children's lives. Take action today! It's only a fiver.

Good for Christine. These are important things to her, and personal. Even more personal, because it was on the front pages towards the end of the year 2009 in that familiar phenomenon we know as tabloid frenzy. The more famous the person, the more frenzied are the tabloids, and Christine's fame was spreading. She was asked to present the teaching-awards show with Jeremy Vine at the Theatre Royal, Drury Lane, 'a glittering event before 2,000 guests'. She and Myleene Klass fronted TV and radio adverts for the Disasters Emergency Committee's appeal in the aftermath of Typhoon Ketsana, which hit the Philippines and parts of Vietnam, and the huge earthquakes that struck western Sumatra. Christine and Adrian hosted the 2010 National Television Awards. Christine was a judge for Children's Champions.

Her smile was everywhere, and now there were rumours that Christine was seeing a Chelsea and England footballer. Possibly a PR expert might have said that she didn't handle the situation as well as she might. She still hadn't quite grasped the extent of her fame and what that implies. Maybe her natural reaction was that it was none of anybody else's business. Maybe she didn't want to be seen as a WAG. Maybe she didn't want to be the cause of more mud being thrown at the footballer, Frank Lampard, who had already attracted much opprobrium for leaving his partner of some years, Elen Rives, and their two children. This was before he met Christine 'at a nightclub', said one paper, and obviously well before they struck up a relationship, but that wouldn't have stopped the speculation. '*One Show* host tempts Frank away from his children'? No, thank you.

As it was, the problem soon became compounded by yet another reprise of the rumour that Christine and Adrian were having a bit of a do. 'Poor Christine Bleakley from *The One Show*. Imagine ending up in a life where you are punished for not finding Adrian Chiles attractive.' Thus wrote a sympathetic critic, summarising a widely held view that, by socialising with a footballer, and a Chelsea one at that, she had upset her recently divorced friend and colleague. Understandably, all the gossipers believed that Adrian found Christine attractive and therefore, as the night follows the day, he must be jealous, seeing Lampard in an association that he himself would give his right arm for.

But what was the association? Let us see how a tabloid newspaper builds a report out of almost nothing. 'Frank Lampard scored a hat-trick on Saturday – but only twice on the football pitch.' Evidence for this: Frank scored two goals as Chelsea beat Blackburn Rovers 5–0, and was seen to be 'very close' to Christine at the Amika nightclub in Kensington. Seen by whom? By someone who worked at the club, so that's a definitely reliable source.

The same source said that they were in a gang of people from *Strictly*, and Frank sat next to Christine. He 'looked smitten'. Hands up, please, all the men who, sitting next to Christine Bleakley, would look bored, uninterested and wishing they were somewhere else.

'I didn't see them kissing,' said the source. So, what else didn't you see them doing?

'There were some outrageous dance moves.' Well, they were all from *Strictly*, contestants and professionals, except Frank, of course, who 'didn't get too involved himself'. No, well, you wouldn't, would you, not in that company. Sensible lad?

'I'm not sure if Frank and Christine left in the same car,' said the source. Thank you, m'lud, and that is the case for the prosecution.

However, the story got hotter, as sources (they're all over the place) 'spotted' the pair of them together during the next two weekends. Christine couldn't even go to Eamonn Holmes's 50th-birthday party at Old Trafford, without it being pointed out that this was where Manchester United played – 'Frank Lampard's Chelsea's arch rivals'. She was photographed smiling while walking along, talking on her mobile. Obviously, this was clear evidence of her being delighted by Frank, whom she had seen the night before.

'I was horrified,' said Christine, 'when people first started saying Adrian and I were having an affair, but for some reason it got legs and started galloping. He is like my brother. We can fight and then everything's forgiven in a few minutes. Those journalists can't accept anything ordinary. You've got to hate each other or be jumping into bed. Until all that started, I'd never seen my name outside the *Belfast Telegraph*.'

And now they were following her and Frank. Claiming not to be very interested in football, and certainly not a WAG, she said, 'I work every day.'

Some of our opinion formers claimed to have noticed tension between the sofa mates, observing an increased fixedness in Christine's smile, while Adrian's grumpiness reached new depths as if a cloud of the sulks were gathered around his head. The advice was clear. Adrian: grow up. Christine: scotch the rumours by coming clean.

Exactly at this time, one of the guests on the show was Professor Robert Winston, who was launching a project examining human nature. As a test for his theories, he had drawn what he claimed was a personality profile of each of the two presenters including, he said, 'the sort of sexual partners Adrian and Christine might have'.

We can imagine millions of viewers suddenly paying full attention, calling in other halves from the kitchen to watch this. Blimey! It was all going to go pear-shaped. Adrian and Christine seemed unprepared for such revelations. The *sort* of sexual partners? What did that mean?

The nation, that is to say the more prurient and crude members thereof, such as most of us, waited for Winston to say that Christine would allow only highly trained, superbly honed athletes into her bed, preferably rich ones who played football for a living. She would never consider dropping her drawers for any beer-swilling, slightly tubby West Brom supporter, especially one who wore a football shirt to matches and introduced television programmes about football, but didn't actually play it.

What would Adrian do when the professor said that, on the other hand, the West Brom supporter in question would yearn for slim beauties with long dark hair, enticing eyes, flashing teeth and smashing figures but was doomed to fail in such a quest?

In the event, Winston proved to be all gong and no dinner. He said nothing to blow the smoking fire into roaring flames. The nation sighed in disappointment.

In truth, the psychology of twin TV hosts is complex. Are they rivals? Are they so generous to each other that rivalry doesn't come into it? Do they praise each other off camera, sympathise in difficulties, criticise when necessary? Is there a dominant one and a subservient one? Why, on the telly anyway, is it always Jack and Jill, and never Jill and Jack (or Jack and Jack apart from Ant and Dec, or Jill and Jill for that matter)? What does it mean when Jill looks admiringly at Jack while he is speaking, yet Jack scratches his nose in apparent boredom while Jill says something from the script? Why is Jack pilloried when he's caught having a quick shufti down Jill's cleavage?

Why does the Richard-and-Judy combo work so well, while the Eammon-and-Anthea dynamic duo turned the milk sour? Which way would Adrian and Christine go?

In a world where entire magazines are devoted to this kind of tittle-tattle, where television is a constant topic of conversation and therefore where its stars are legitimate targets for innuendo, the more you try to hide something, the more interest is generated and the more inconvenient it can all become.

Ah, well, the winter arrived and with it evidence on our screens of an entirely unforeseen consequence of global warming. The more perceptive of *The One Show*'s audience began to notice a strange, lichen-like growth on Adrian's finely chiselled features. Was he attempting to reinvent himself as a trendy singleton? Did he think designer stubble would succeed with the ladies, where currently his smooth cheeks were failing? But it wasn't designer stubble, was it? It was a beard.

This was a considerable advance on his previous hairy adventure, when he allowed a few days' growth to go unimpeded in January 2008, ready to be shaved at the viewers' request by an Italian barber from the Dorchester Hotel with a cut-throat razor. Then, he had complained that he was itching like a man in a fuzzy tree. No, this was much more serious than that.

It is a fact of bearded life that there are three sorts of men. One is the chap with steel wool in his cheeks, who can produce almost overnight a mass of black, red, brown or white curly stuff of Brillo pad texture, which can be left to grow rampantly or sculpted like topiary to any shape its owner desires. We think of the actor James Robertson Justice, or one of those statues of ancient Assyrian kings, or a Russian hat made of Persian lamb.

Two is the fellow whose beard is ruled by gravity. Long hairs grow straight downwards and can be left for good or trimmed into well-behaved triangles – think Saruman the White, Salvador Dalí, or anybody called Van Dyck. Three is the bumfluff merchant, the poor lad who, whatever he does, ends up looking like a badly sheared Angora goat. The hair grows willy-nilly, in patches, as if parts of the ground are fertile but others are dry and overshadowed by trees.

Adrian, alas, belonged in the third group. He simply

did not suit a beard for a start, and it wasn't a Robertson Justice or a Saruman; and sitting next to the angelic, radiant, Gloria in Excelsis that is Christine Bleakley only served to emphasise the rule that some chops are best without hair. Of course, if Christine had been on the sofa with Basil Brush or Roland Rat, she would still have been the angelic, radiant et cetera, which, in a way, seemed to work in *The One Show*'s favour when she was positioned next to Adrian the Barber's Nightmare.

The worse the beard became, the more viewers tuned in. At one point, more than 7 million were gazing in fascination at the silken perfection that is Christine's loveliness, next to Birmingham's answer to the Honey Monster. BBC executives apparently did not see things in a favourable light. They thought that if Adrian didn't look so untidy, as if he'd lost his razor and couldn't work out where to get another, ratings would be 8 million.

Even when Adrian was awarded Beard of the Winter by the Beard Liberation Front (BLF), it didn't soften the hearts of those BBC functionaries whose offices have large windows but, for the moment anyway, they were powerless to do anything. Here is what we might call the official view of beards in the early twenty-first century, from the style and grooming expert Jodie Harrison: 'I've noticed a new resurgence in beard wearing. It has become fashionable again in media and music circles. Beards can look great but they have to be well maintained and they have to be part of a whole look – they shouldn't be scruffy.'

Ah, well, yes, but you see, the two phrases 'part of a whole look' and 'Adrian dressed for work' do not appear to be closely linked. What, Mr Chiles might ask, is a whole look? He thought he had a look. That was why a survey had found that viewers thought Chiles was TV's scruffiest.

'I'd got the beard going but it wasn't great and I was just about to shave it off in our make-up room when Kirsty Young told me to leave it on. Since then Davina McCall has told me she liked it.' And you can be sure that Mesdames Young and McCall would never dream of having a little jest at your expense, can't you, Adrian?

Socialist historian, letter writer and founder of the BLF Keith Flett, said that people such as BBC mandarins don't trust beard wearers. 'They will tolerate Noel Edmonds wearing a beard for an entertainment programme, but they frown on news or current affairs presenters being hirsute, unless they are only on the radio.'

There were huge arguments in the papers, emails flew about, bloggers blogged, opinions were expressed by the thousand. Here are just a few, from web pages supervised by the motor journalist Robin Brown:

As a human being I cannot help but recoil in horror at the reddish monstrosity nesting on his face. To my eyes he looks like an arctic explorer, lost and feral, forced to feed on the blubber from a whale carcass. [. . .]

Come on Chiles, have a shave. You look a mess, man. Far from the intended rugged, it's more hungover bear. [. . .]

Flicked to MOTD2 during break in the snooker – aaaargh. Adrian Chiles has a beard. He looks like a homeless Henry VIII. [. . .]

Adrian Chiles's beard makes him look like the violent alcoholic captain of a Victorian steamship. [. . .]

He looks like the leader of his own cult. Is he kipping on that sofa?

Other comments included 'crap in orange on a chubby bloke', 'a battered old armchair instead of a head', 'even more like a scrotum'. On the bright side, it was pointed out that 'it would take Lampard months to grow anything like that', and more complimentary viewers said that Adrian looked like Kenneth Branagh in *Wallander* and an Ewok from *Return of the Jedi*.

Sport Relief was the eventual beneficiary, with an enthusiastic Christine slapping foam all over to the music of a Mexican band, finishing off with a small portable electric shaver, and leaving the embarrassed and bemused Adrian clearly planning a visit to a proper de-bearding emporium, perhaps the Dorchester Hotel.

Despite all the fun and games, and 7 million viewers for *The One Show*, and smiles all round, and studio guests like Sir Michael Caine and Dame Helen Mirren, there was, figuratively speaking, a dark cloud on the horizon or, should we say, a gingery kind of a cloud.

CHAPTER EIGHT
OFF TO ITV

When Wayne Rooney left Everton, he had to dump all his previous loyalties to that club, including boyhood worship to the extent of turning his bedroom at home into a holy blue sepulchre. All of a sudden, he had to reincarnate as a Manchester United player, red throughout. Meanwhile, all those football supporters at Everton, who had idolised Rooney and sung his praises to the skies, had to adjust their opinions, hopes and dreams, not to mention their language, to transform a talented teenager from prodigy to enemy, brackets, useless.

Something similar occurs when icons of the BBC switch to ITV, accompanied by loadsamoney. The difference, of course, is that Rooney could also have gone to Chelsea, Arsenal, Barcelona, Real Madrid, Man City or whoever was big enough and had the dosh – and still *could* go to one of them. But there is only one ITV.

Looking at the situation coldly, you can see why ITV wanted to improve their early-morning ratings to attract more advertisers and better advertising rates. GMTV was losing ground to BBC1 and had been doing so for a couple of years, with audiences falling from 1.5 million to 800,000 while the BBC climbed to 1.4 million. The GMTV brand, launched in 1993, had been subject to a root-and-branch review since ITV took full control in November 2009, buying the 25 per cent it did not already own from Disney for £22.5 million.

On the production side, editor Martin Frizzell was replaced by Ian Rumsey. Off air, GMTV the company also disappeared as a corporate entity, with the GMTV Limited being renamed ITV Breakfast Limited. So something had to be done, and an announcement was made that, indeed, something *would* be done, but what? Like the football manager who looks at his reserves and his youth team, fails to see the starry striker he needs to improve results and so goes to the market, the ITV bosses could see no saviours on their books at that time.

There would be no shortage of applicants if the various jobs in presenting a new-format GMTV were advertised. That was not the problem. You'd have a queue of beauty queens down the street wanting to be weather girl, hoping that would translate into something better, and another queue of already slightly famous people wanting to get in front of a camera, any camera, each believing that his or her special blend of personality, charm, looks and wit was exactly that for which the nation was yearning. The difficulty would be in identifying potential, always hard to do, and so you can't blame the ITV bosses for preferring to buy something ready made with, as they say, a proven track record.

Behind the scenes, there must have been talks about talks. Different people would have been suggested in meetings, and agents would have been sounded out. Channels Four and Five would have been combed as well as the BBC. Executives with power in their hands but no notions in their heads would have brainstormed all over the place until there was hardly a brain cell left that wasn't shipwrecked, while the good folk already doing the job soldiered on, with rumours in the press filling their minds with doubts and uncertainties.

In the event, all the writhings and reelings of ITV managers became pointless, when a decision made in the BBC set the juggernaut a-rolling. Someone, maybe the Fat Controller or She Who Must Be Obeyed, had the idea of putting Chris Evans on the Friday edition of *The One Show*. He used to do a show on a Friday, remember? *TFI Friday*, on Channel Four? It lasted four or five years, and very good it was, although, like most shows relying entirely on a presenter's appeal, it faded eventually. And then he went on to *OFI Sunday*, on big brother ITV, which lasted five episodes.

Don't remember that? What did the F stand for?

Well, with 7 million viewers and all the goodwill that implied, you can't help wondering why BBC executives, no less inept (or no more ept, anyway) than their ITV equivalents, would want to mend a machine that wasn't even making a slight grinding noise. Likewise, you cannot help but wonder what said executives imagined the reaction of Adrian and Christine would be. By this time, they *were The One Show*. They loved doing it. It was not a complete broadcasting life in itself, but that meant it left time and space for other things. Another BBC press release said, 'Adrian is one of the BBC's most versatile and admired presenters'.

Viewing figures were the envy of many, so, tell you what, let's really upset Adrian and Christine by bringing in the ginger monster to do *TFI Friday* all over again.

Upset? Why would it upset them? Adrian won't mind.

Scuttlebut abounded. The showbiz and celeb specialists on the newspapers and magazines were scrabbling about for gossip. 'The BBC wants to ditch Adrian Chiles from *The One Show* on Fridays, so they can turn it into a hour-long star-studded spectacular,' said the *News of the World*.

The *Daily Express* carried a story saying that the BBC wanted to sideline Adrian, even lose him altogether, and was briefing against him as part of the new strategy to change the format of the show. Chiles was, said an insider, grumpy all the time and liable to throw tantrums. Another insider, presumably one on the other side of inside, said, 'BBC1 is tinkering with a successful show for no good reason. Everyone is fed up. They've already got rid of one of the two editors. The other has been given his notice. He's going to be replaced by an editor from *Panorama* to make it a more factual show. They plan to strip out all the show-business items and move them to the Friday show for Chris Evans.'

Hardly anyone mentioned the last time Chris Evans attempted to add a Friday night TV show to five days a week on the steam wireless. He resigned on air, on Radio 1, after BBC managers told him they wouldn't let him do the telly too.

After years on *Drivetime* on Radio 2, the bespectacled, manic hero of *Don't Forget Your Toothbrush* was deemed to have reached the maturity his 44 years might have led one to expect, rather than being the 'self-important twat', as he described himself, that he appeared to be when he did his broadcast resignation. And so, after months of speculation, the news was out at last. BBC executives definitely wanted Evans to take over from Adrian on Fridays on *The One Show*.

The business plan specified that the new, hour-long Friday transmissions would concentrate less on the Reithian inform and educate and more on the third priority, entertain. Indeed, as *TFI Friday* had been, '*TOS Friday*' was to be the start of the weekend, and it was to start it 'with a bang'. It was not clear how this would affect the other four shows in the week. Would they be less entertaining?

If, as some pundits claimed, the move had been knocking about BBC corridors since the autumn, more or less since ITV bought GMTV (coincidence, obviously), it certainly seemed to take Adrian by surprise. He would quit. No, he wouldn't quit. Yes, he would quit. Negotiations were taking place. More money. More shows. Don't care, still going to quit.

'It is understood Chiles is likely to stay, although he is yet to sign a new BBC deal,' said the *Guardian*. 'A deal has been agreed for Chris to do Fridays,' said a BBC insider. 'There has been a lot of talking about what happens if entertainment is saved for Fridays, but the fact is that Adrian will not be required.'

A BBC spokeswoman said, 'While we do not discuss contracts, Adrian is part of our plans for the future of *The One Show*.' Which was nice.

Another spokesperson said, 'Adrian Chiles is currently talking to the BBC.'

Adrian, already known to some as Mr Grumpy, was

said to be threatening to quit the BBC altogether. BBC bosses could see only Friday, A-list celebs, showbiz, and 'Help! Jonathan Ross is going!', and they did not associate the recently bearded one with that scene.

A BBC source said, 'Adrian knows the best guests will be targeted at the Friday show. He'll do the spade work and miss out on the glory. It's not fair. They'd be crazy to lose Adrian.'

The One Show had become a national treasure, and the BBC was messing about with it. It was among the corporation's highest-rated programmes, with a regular audience of more than 5 million viewers, and sometimes more than 7 million.

'I think Adrian Chiles is a brilliant presenter,' said Esther Rantzen, a lady well qualified to comment on Adrian, having presented *Nationwide* and *That's Life*, and being in possession of a fine set of teeth. 'It's not that I don't like Christine. I think she's very good but I think that Adrian is outstanding.' And we're sure Christine would say the same about you, Esther.

The show's cheeriness, in among all the serious gloom of everyday existence, had been a shining light. It was warm, it was not cynical or clever-dicky, and there was always a smile and a good laugh somewhere along the way. When the studio staff joined in the laughter, it seemed real enough. It was all so genuine, no easy feat for TV folk, when the basic situation – of a person talking to a camera – is itself unreal. So, when Christine got busy with the wax on Adrian's chest hair, it was like a party game at home. Being able to make viewers believe that had been – funnily enough – something that Chris Evans was once known for.

Now, said one, Adrian had laid down the law. It was to be five nights or nothing. Another source, supposedly inside the Beeb, stated as fact that Adrian had been offered a new and massive deal, including a BBC2 topical comedy (although in what capacity was not defined), alongside all the other stuff he did such as *Match of the Day 2* and, for as long as my Lord of Sugar or Sir A N Other would keep firing, Adrian's long-stop programme *The Apprentice: You're Fired!*. With all this, it was confidently asserted, it was just not possible for him to do five episodes a week of *The One Show*. So that was why Evans was being brought in – to ease the burden on Adrian.

Adrian apparently insisted that he could cope, but the BBC remained firm. They simply had to have the ginger nut on a Friday, and, if Adrian didn't like that, they knew someone who would. Chris Hollins was well thought of on breakfast television and had gathered a throng of fans with his performance on *Strictly Come Dancing*. His throng was nowhere near as big as Adrian's throng, but the other Chris, Evans, was not negotiable.

Possibly another ingredient in the BBC's stubbornness was the inability of anyone there to define exactly why *The One Show* was so popular, and they were not alone in that. One commentator wrote:

For those who do not watch *The One Show*, the amount of coverage devoted to Adrian Chiles's threat to leave the BBC programme if he is replaced by Chris Evans on Fridays, has been astonishing. This is basically a story about a man with a rather grumpy demeanour who may leave a television programme that regularly contains dangerous levels of Gyles Brandreth – but it's being treated like the death of a minor royal. We never got anything like this when Bill Oddie left *Springwatch*.

For the media to make a fuss, there has to be a certain level of interest among the populace. Redtops and numerous magazines would not devote words and pictures by the zillion to soap-opera actors and footballers' wives if there weren't a market for it. Similarly, slowly but surely, *The One Show* had crept into the national consciousness and lodged there, and made a home there. When Adrian grew his beard, it was news. When Carol Thatcher said 'golliwog' it was news because of where she said it and with whom, and who she was at the time – a *One Show* reporter.

When the possibility was mooted that Adrian and Christine were collaborating in the rumpy-pumpy department, it was the talk of every town. But why?

If you analysed *The One Show*, you would have progressed to nowhere. Ask the producers and the stars why they followed a piece about allotments with a story about an orphan baby ostrich, then something on the Battle of Killiecrankie with an interview with a man talking about EC regulations on sherbet lemons, they would say because people liked it that way. Ask people why they liked it that way, and you would not get a scientifically valid answer.

Ask why they kept their celeb guests in view all the time, and why they asked celebs questions on subjects about which they clearly knew nothing, and they'd say it's a bit of fun.

As we have already said, Christine believed that viewers at that time of day don't want anything too stressful. She might have added that a certain security helps too. Once a formula has proved a success, people want it to stay like that. They want to feel that they can turn the telly on and get exactly what they expect to get, which includes surprises, eye openers and trivia. That's the sort of thing that *The One Show* did every day.

Or perhaps there was not much else on at that time. Rather than read a book, make a model of the Blackpool Tower out of toothpicks or take the dog for a walk, and rather than watch *Emmerdale* or *Channel 4 News*, you were happy with *The One Show*. And why not?

Clearly, the presenters were central. They looked casual on their sofa, liking each other, liking the viewers, and being like the viewers. Adrian, in one critic's words, 'never fails to give the impression of a Black Country labourer who has wandered into a television studio and doesn't realise the camera is on'. Christine and Adrian together were approachable family friends.

If only the clever people in charge of television could write down precisely why we like what we do, and predict just how much we shall like it, there would never be any TV flops. Let us not underestimate the difficulty here, when you have such a diverse animal as the human race and wish to predict its behaviour while being educated, informed and entertained.

I watched *The One Show* and looked on in disgust at Adrian Chiles eating a rabbit pie. Has that heathen never heard of Good Friday, and abstaining from eating meat. It just highlights the morons that edit the show, or not as the case may be. I am not a religious person, however protocol should be observed. Is Chiles's next plan of attack to whistle at 11.00 am on Armistice day, while eating a meat pie. Chiles is a disgrace, as well as the 2 clowns who helped him.

I am totally disgusted with the bunch of baboons who run BBC, the same lot who pays Jonathan Ross £6 million of our money and let him offend people, and then pat him on the back. Hypocrital Idiots.

As for them 2 idiots who present *The One Show*, they along with the Producer, should be sacked. Bring on Chris Evans.

Well, there you are. Baboons, clowns, morons, and 'hypocrital' idiots. Or, on the other hand:

I really enjoy *The One Show*; however, it has to be said that when Adrian and Christine are away something is truly lost. For a starter – the programme becomes BORING!! Whether you call it chemistry or something else – but these two presenters – TOGETHER – really make the show. I have nothing against Chris Evans; his energy is great, but why do the BBC always mess with things when clearly everything is fine just the way it is!! Take note BBC (though I don't expect you will!) – you will ruin the format completely if you start interfering. Adrian and Christine are brilliant together. Chris Evans and Christine, umm, well – no, I can't see it personally. I'm always fascinated by the faces Ade and Christine pull whilst their co-presenter is talking – nothing short of gurning sometimes. But – please, please, spare us Chris Evans' almost perpetual grinning and manic babbling. He should come with a health warning – serious irritant. Does he have friends in high places at the BBC or are they just trying to decimate their viewing and listening figures? *The One Show* may be seen by some as being a bit bland but it is an oasis of calm before the storm that is about to engulf it.

So, all that needs to be done is to reconcile these points of view, or perhaps decide which is the view of the majority – or, even more radical for senior executives, take note, as recommended in that comment. Then, everything on telly would succeed according to its own objectives. Nothing would be broken, so nothing would need fixing. Ah, but, you see, just as when you hire regulators in Brussels they will always find something to regulate, so, if you have executives and administrators in charge of something creative and inspirational, that runs perfectly smoothly without their interference, those executives and administrators will not rest until they have found a way of interfering, or improving the product, as they might call it.

Christine did not need improving. Her sister Nicola, who achieved her own 15 minutes of fame by conquering an eating problem and losing seven stone in a year and being crowned Northern Ireland's Slimmer of the Year, said, 'Everybody's so proud of her – our parents, our friends, she's really flying the flag for Northern Ireland. She hasn't changed and never will. She's a real home girl. She loves her job but she also loves getting breakfast at our mum and dad's. We talk on the phone ten times a day.'

Another frequent caller was Chelsea footballer Frank Lampard, acknowledged by now and taken to Belfast (not to meet the parents, as elsewhere reported) and seen, or rather 'spotted', while 'laughing' as they 'enjoyed themselves' in a city-centre bar. Laughing? Enjoying themselves? Whatever next?

The paparazzi were never off the hunt, which is the price of fame these days, snapping her as she left his house, or him as he left the pub after a drink (sorry, a 'romantic lunch') with Christine. Christine said she couldn't believe all the interest. Maybe, despite what we said earlier, she hadn't quite adjusted yet to the life rather more public than that of a floor manager made teatime TV presenter.

Once the story appeared as confirmed in the press, the usual load of nonsense also appeared on the comment pages of the Web.

I bet he's as dull as ditchwater. That's certainly how he comes across on the television. Poor Christine.

I don't know what the attraction is with Christine Bleakley. Nice figure but not good looking and that accent grates on my nerves. She doesn't let the grass grow under her feet. She has gone down in my estimation if she fancies being a Wag. Maybe she's

> jealous of Cheryl. Lampard will need ear plugs if he
> has to put up with her voice for long.

> Come on, Christine. He looks a right miserable
> man.

Miserable-looking maybe, but Christine seemed happy
and was fully at ease in the company of Frank's family –
sisters Natalie and Claire and father Frank, mother Pat
having died in 2008 – as at the Football Writers' awards
when Frank had the Tribute prize.

When you're a star, my girl, irritating newshounds and
Internet insults come with the stardom. They are part of
the package. If the papers don't have anything factual to
report, they'll make it up, or twist it. It's the big downside
of being a personality.

'I read an article that said I was overambitious, seeking
world domination and the overturn of Cheryl Cole. It was
all the opposite of what I am. It was lies. Upsetting lies,'
Christine said.

A less upsetting journalist malfunction was that she
and Frank met in a nightclub. According to Piers Morgan,
and he should know, it wasn't a nightclub where they
met. It was a bar at the Grosvenor House Hotel, where
celebrities, both major and minor, were having a drink
and a chat after the Pride of Britain awards. Mr Lampard
espied Miss Bleakley looking lovely, and asked Mr
Morgan if he knew her. 'Very well,' was the reply. 'So
what's she like?' enquired Frank. 'Brainy, funny and, as
you can see, very pretty and so, as such, much too good
for a Chelsea footballer.' Piers introduced them anyway
and left them to talk. The pair of them should be warned

that Mr Morgan as matchmaker has previous. He claims to have introduced Paul McCartney to Heather Mills.

Perhaps, though, Christine and Frank were more of a match. She is much overqualified as a WAG, but Frank has nine GCSEs, which is more than some football teams have between them.

'He is known for being intelligent,' said Christine, 'and obviously I'm very happy with that. I need conversation. I don't mean I want an intellectual. Just somebody who is smart, and he is.'

Speaking of smartness, appearing on Reeves and Mortimer's *Shooting Stars* can be a bit of a backhanded compliment. They like to have a good-looking girl sitting next to the lugubrious Jack Dee, but the girl knows she's going to get some stick from Vic Reeves. You don't do the show unless you believe you can take it and, back in August 2009, Christine's test had been a good deal more vulgar than most. Balancing a pork pie on her head would have seemed tame. Maybe she was getting away with it after all. But no. After standing on the desk before her, rubbing his knees in that uniquely coarse fashion, Vic jumped to the floor and, after Christine had given him a surprise kiss, from which he took a moment to recover, offered to show her his tattoo. This turned out to be a crude drawing of a face, supposedly Christine's, on his lower back. Revealing it also showed very grubby underpants with grotesquely enhanced skid marks. He'd had it done for her especially, he said – to which Christine asked, 'Which bit?' – and threatened her with his front-of-body version, a chap with a beard and a sausage in his mouth. Christine, game girl, was almost speechless with laughter and was probably pleased that, whatever Vic Reeves did, it could have been so much worse.

She was voted favourite guest of the series by Bob Mortimer. He said she'd shown a side of herself that nobody knew existed. Possibly *Shooting Stars* is the kind of programme that does that to a girl.

There was also *Sport Relief* on BBC1, on which Gary Lineker, James Corden, Richard Hammond, Claudia Winkleman, Fearne Cotton, Davina McCall and Patrick Kielty hosted 'a full Friday night's worth of brilliant *Sport Relief* television' with, of course, our Christine.

The evening featured special appearances from celebrity guests, music performances and a chance to see the highlights of the celebrity challenges from Christine Bleakley – water-skiing across the Channel – *Blue Peter*'s Helen Skelton and the Sport Relief Million Pound Bike Ride, which included David Walliams, Miranda Hart, Jimmy Carr and Russell Howard.

There was a one-off 'golftastic' edition of *Ashes to Ashes*, featuring sporting and entertainment legends from the eighties, and the *Outnumbered* family also featured in their own show, as they prepared to take part in the Sport Relief Mile. And *Gavin and Stacey*'s Smithy (James Corden), fresh from training the England football team on Red Nose Day, gave his unique sporting advice to more sporting heroes.

This was the kind of company Christine was keeping now. Maybe she didn't need that Adrian Chiles after all. Back home she was still a cherished VIP:

Join a host of stars from the worlds of sport and showbiz and take part in this year's Sport Relief

Mile at Custom House Square in Belfast on Sunday 16 March. BBC Northern Ireland's own Christine Bleakley has just signed up and will be taking time out of her busy schedule presenting *The One Show*. Christine will be joining local sports stars including boxer Brian Magee, the Northern Ireland Ladies Netball Team and World Masters Heptathlon Champion Geraldine Finnegan. Players from local soccer, GAA and rugby teams will also be lending their support.

Current Miss GB, Gemma Garrett from Belfast, will also be taking the Sport Relief challenge along with familiar faces from local TV screens including Denise Watson and Jackie Fullerton from Sport, and Rigsy from ATL TV.

On this subject Christine, looking very nice in a white Sport Relief T-shirt, said: 'I'm really looking forward to getting back to Belfast and taking part in the Sport Relief Mile. There has been a fantastic turnout in previous years so I expect to be joining hundreds of people starting from Custom House Square on 16 March. The great thing about the mile is that you don't have to be super-fit – anyone can do it. It's going to be great fun so I'm looking forward to seeing everyone there.

Belfast was one of 23 flagship Sport Relief Miles taking place across the UK on that day. Live coverage from the Mile events was shown on BBC1.

In the first half of 2010, Christine appeared on six TV shows that were not her own: the National Television Awards, *Chris Moyles' Quiz Night*, Children's Champion

Awards, *Michael Winner's Dining Stars*, *Rev*, and *BBC Breakfast*.

For the Children's Champions, the celebrity panel of judges included Sarah Brown, Emma Bunton, Peter Andre, Dame Kelly Holmes, Jayne Torvill, Christopher Dean, Angela Griffin and Christine, who chose the winners from nominations made by members of the public. A teacher, a school dinner lady, a doctor, a nurse, a hospital cleaner, a member of the emergency services, a foster mum – these were the kinds of unsung heroes across the country who received recognition, with all the accompanying razzmatazz that's the exact opposite of what they usually do.

In the Winner show, the important, world-famous and hugely charismatic film director and restaurant critic, doing a very creditable imitation of a creature previously unknown to evolution (being a cross between Alan Sugar and a smooth newt), visited four lots of 'ordinary people' who, for some unaccountable reason, had volunteered to cook a meal for him. The best-performing cooks would be invited *chez* Winner and his fabulous kitchen, to prepare a meal for a table of celebs including Roger Moore, Andrew Neil, Giorgio Locatelli and our Christine, who could hardly get a word in edgeways.

In the first episode of Series Two of the Moyles programme, the contestants to join Chris were David Walliams, Peter Andre and Christine Bleakley. Each had to play for their fans in the audience, winning them a share of not very much money. The share depended on how many people backed the winning star. In this show, 34 per cent of the audience thought that Peter Andre would win, with only 11 per cent backing Christine. The audience was right. Andre went through to the final.

Rev was a comedy sitcom series based on the everyday parish frustrations and accompanying spiritual and moral conflicts of the Rev. Adam Smallbone. In the first episode, after a rumour that his local C of E school had been given top star rating by the Ofsted inspectors, his church filled up with newly fervent parent worshippers hoping to get their angelic offspring into said school. By the fourth episode, the Reverend Smallbone was moving into *Father Ted* territory and believing himself suitable for a career in the media. He managed an appearance on *The One Show*, where, interviewed by Christine and Adrian (no acting required, then), he made some unwise remarks about the church and homosexuality.

The previous year there had been only two guest appearances, *Shooting Stars* and *Would I Lie to You?*, the programme that bears a remarkable resemblance to the veteran show *Call My Bluff*, except that the subject matter is the panellists' supposed deepest secrets rather than strange words scraped from the bottom of the dictionary. Christine danced with host Rob Brydon and easily fooled the opposition with her story of picking all the red M&Ms out of the bowl for a *Coronation Street* actor, when she was a floor manager.

Before that, there had been the single episode of *Ready Steady Cook*, soon after her beginnings on *The One Show*, in September 2007. Thus rises the star – from a daft afternoon cooking show with Ainsley Harriott to a daft early-evening cooking show with Michael Winner. Such are the trials of celebrity.

And then you find yourself the subject of a Debra Stephenson and Jon Culshaw impression, and your name appears on Caroline Aherne's forehead in *The Royle*

Family Christmas Special. When Patrick Kielty accidentally revealed Christine's mobile-phone number on air, she received hundreds of texts, and not one nasty one. They were all warning her to change her number.

But her best friends remain old ones, from Belfast days, far away from the London celeb circuit. One is a teacher and one is a doctor and the third is her sister Nicola. They are nothing to do with the glitter of TV, and Christine herself is not in its thrall either. She says she is not 'high-maintenance', and has 'a housewife inside me, trying to get out'.

Christine's cross-Channel water-skiing was a great deal more serious and much more than just a fund-raising stunt. It was the first time that anyone had done it. There had been crossings by pedalo, jet ski, amphibious car, even pedal-powered aircraft, but no water-skiing, much less by a young woman who admits to more than a passing fear of water – which might explain why she's not so hot at swimming.

'I was in a swimming pool on holiday and I went under the water and my dad pulled me out and managed to get me back to life again. And I haven't gone near the water ever since. [Yes you have, Christine: you went surfing, remember?] I can swim about one length and that's it so I've had to overcome a lot of personal fears.

'People say, "Oh, you're skiing across? Fantastic. What fun." Well, it's not. Frank thinks I'm mad. The strain on arms and legs, and lower back, it's incredible. I've had to hit that gym to reconstruct my muscles. I mean, come on, I sit on a sofa for a living. But look at my arms now. They're like tree trunks. I look like Popeye. As soon as this is over I'm going back to being girly Christine.'

Just how it would be over, in failure or success, Christine had her doubts. 'I've done most of my training on a lake. Out at sea it's a bit different. I did learn to surf a few years ago for a TV show in Northern Ireland, but the waves here are going in the other direction.' Hmm, well, we think it's probably you going in the other direction, Christine, but never mind. We get the point.

'I think of Hajara in Uganda every day. I have a picture of her and her family on my computer, so that, when I come into the office exhausted and hating water-skiing and everything to do with it, I can remind myself about certain things that matter.'

She did the 22 miles from Dover to Calais in one hour forty minutes, and fell in eight, nine or ten times, depending on who was counting.

'It was freezing,' she said. 'You see these huge ships coming past you. A lonely experience, especially when the swell stops you seeing anything at all, including the boat that's pulling you. Every muscle is aching and I just cried a river.' Perhaps the specimen of pond life who wrote, 'Methinks Ms Bleakley's publicity machine has got above itself' would like to try something similar.

'Having to get up after every fall was exhausting, but I'd talked about it, trained for it. So I had to do it.'

Gale-force winds had meant cancelling the attempt twice and the sea was still rather lumpy. She fell off at least seven times before the halfway mark, and falling into the Channel at twenty miles an hour feels not dissimilar to being tackled at full speed by a rugby league forward.

She raised more than £250,000 for charity, and described the trip as 'utter torture. Halfway through I thought, I can't do this, because everything was starting to give. I had a searing pain in my lower back, my legs were starting to wobble, and my hands – I just couldn't hold on any longer. But I managed to get the strength from somewhere and I can't quite believe I've done it.'

Christine had been through months of training with Professor Gregory Whyte, Olympic pentathlete and the resource of choice for celebs who decide they're going to do something silly and physical for charity, such as David Walliams swimming the Channel in 2006. Said Christine, 'On my first day of training I thought the water was freezing, which shows you how little I knew, and I managed two minutes of water-skiing and I was knackered. I decided I would go home, think about it, and chicken out the next morning. But I didn't. Professor Whyte knows all about Channel swimming. From the training he made me do, I think he was expecting me to get lost and have to swim at least half of it.'

Adrian was in close support on a nice dry boat, shouting ironic encouragement through a loud hailer, as he would, but churning inside for the bravery of his best-loved sofa friend. As one commentator almost put it:

> While skiing for twenty two miles
> Young Christine was beaming her smiles.
> At Calais, quite vexed
> She saw what came next –
> A smacker from Adrian Chiles.

Guardian blogger Stuart Heritage said:

Water-skiing across the English channel was a make-or-break moment for Christine Bleakley.

Succeed and she'd be lauded as a hero, but fail and she'd be doomed to only be remembered as the woman who started crying because she couldn't hold on to a bit of rope for very long. But, magnificently, Bleakley triumphed on Friday, beating all the odds – as a water-skiing novice who couldn't swim and met with less than ideal conditions, even her own trainer appeared to doubt the likelihood of success – and raising lots of cash for Sport Relief in the process.

Very nice Stuart, and we know the *Guardian* is frightfully PC, but we are sure Christine would rather be a heroine than a hero.

Anyway, she was invited to Number Ten to receive personal congratulations from Prime Minister Gordon Brown, who called her inspiring – and quite right, too. We must pause for a moment here, to imagine Gordon Brown being inspired to water-ski across the Channel. Or, if we were to be politically even-handed, Eric Pickles water-skiing across the Channel. No. Stop it. That's quite enough. Ann Widdecombe?

Adrian had already done his bit, cycling 335 miles in two days with Alan Shearer, from St James's Park, Newcastle, via The Hawthorns to BBC Television Centre, London. Setting off, Alan, who had met AIDS victims in Uganda, said, 'It'll be one hell of a test.' Adrian, who had been to talk to orphans in Liberia, said, 'I'll have their faces in my mind as we slave up hill and down dale.' They raised £371,065 for Sport Relief. 'I don't know if you can have a transplant of the bones in your bum, but, if you can, I want one,' said Adrian.

Like many celebrities, Adrian and Christine have been involved with Children in Need. For example, in November 2009, Adrian went in the stocks in Swansea. The local paper reported that he could not fail to forget his visit, but probably meant that he could not fail to remember it. First, he was locked in the stocks and had a pile of wet sponges hurled at him, after viewers of *The One Show* voted for him to be thus splatted by the charity's mascot Pudsey Bear and a gang of helpers, as part of a special stunt at the city's Waterfront Winterland.

Adrian said he was freezing cold even before any sponges were thrown. He said, 'There can't be much on telly tonight. People have turned up in their hundreds, if not thousands.' After Father Christmas tipped a bucket of slime over his head, Adrian didn't say much at all.

Christine expected a similar fate in Belfast, where traders from all over the world had come for one of the most popular Christmas events on the whole island of Ireland, the Christmas Continental Market at City Hall. More than 750,000 people had visited the Market in 2008 and 2009 was going to be even bigger. *The One Show* would be broadcasting a Children in Need special stunt, they said, live from the Santa's Grotto, 'when presenter Christine Bleakley will be trying to avoid being gunged by Pudsey and some young local helpers'.

And now, the news we were all waiting for. We read it in our papers on 19 April 2010. *The One Show* and *Match of the Day 2* presenter Adrian Chiles had quit the BBC to join ITV in a four-year deal. He would take up roles with GMTV and ITV's World Cup football coverage. And Christine Bleakley had been voted the world's 85th sexiest woman by readers of the magazine *FHM*, a mere 84 places behind Cheryl Cole.

Adrian's nose was undoubtedly put out of joint by the recruitment of the ginger knob to *TOS*'s Friday airing, and admitted that he had been having 'an awkward period' at the Beeb. 'The chance to front ITV's football coverage and GMTV would have been hard to resist in any case but, coming as it did at an awkward period, it made the decision a bit easier.'

He insisted that he would have been happy to stay, doing the same shows on the same terms, 'especially *The One Show*, of which I am so proud, having worked on it since the first pilots four years ago'.

Who was to blame for turning the world upside down? The papers all pointed the finger at BBC1 controller Jay Hunt and director of vision Jana Bennett. In turn, BBC spokespersons let it be known that there had been development work on a chat show for Adrian, and a panel game, extra to the package that included four nights on *The One Show*, plus *The Apprentice: You're Fired!*, *Match of the Day 2* and other sporting events.

Jay Hunt subsequently said she had had 'extensive talks' with Chiles. He was 'hurt' by her plans to rejuvenate Friday nights after Jonathan Ross had gone, by signing Chris Evans to present *The One Show* on that day. 'I am not in the habit of telling talent to put up with it when I make changes. I spent a lot of time talking to Adrian, but, if a presenter decides to go for a lot of money to another broadcaster, we are not in the business of trying to make huge counteroffers.'

Jana Bennett said that she had hoped that Adrian would have looked at the different types of project on the table. 'I have always been a fan. Talent in this industry does move around. Football was a big attraction from ITV. The Friday question was a big decision, to do with rethinking Friday altogether, not just *The One Show*. We wanted to bring in different types of entertainment on a Friday and Chris Evans was someone I really wanted to have.'

At this time there was no talk of *Daybreak*, although it was known that ITV was planning an overhaul of the breakfast show, with director of daytime and factual Alison Sharman leading the project, she who was seen as responsible for the rebirth and growth of BBC daytime telly while she was there. However, Adrian was a definite for leading ITV's World Cup coverage in June, later the Champions League matches and various other football occasions. He would also be on the *GMTV* sofa five days a week, although it was not clear how room would be made for him, and there was talk of a factual series.

ITV had been in discussions with Adrian for some time, a year or maybe two, and, when the Ginger Ultimatum was announced, they pounced, led by the ITV director of television, channels and online, Peter Fincham, Adrian's old friend and boss from the very start of *The One Show* when he was BBC1 controller.

Fincham said, 'Adrian is a brilliant presenter, journalist and a football fanatic. I am looking forward to working with him again when he joins ITV. He has the rare talent of making television presenting look effortless. He will be at home at ITV whether it is on our flagship breakfast programme or in the football studio.'

A BBC spokesman said, 'We would like to thank

Adrian for his contributions to his programmes and we wish him well for the future.'

Well, thanks, Mr BBC Spokesman. On the subject of effortless TV presenting, we should take note of the comic writer, broadcaster and *Newswipe* host Charlie Brooker's first experience of doing it live. He wet himself (only a little bit), he sweated buckets, he became 'a human-shaped cloud of screaming nerves', and could only wonder at the coolness of some professionals.

According to Charlie Booker, 'Appearing on live TV 'does very strange things to your brain. Having lived through the experience, I can now only assume that every single one of the nation's favourite live telly faces has the ice-blooded personality of a long-range military sniper. That nice Christine Bleakley? Bet she could emotionlessly blast a hole through your forehead while linking to a report on wind farms.'

Sniper or no, it had all happened quite quickly for Adrian, and the actual events were spun a little by those who perhaps were beginning to realise their mistake. Adrian felt that the past was being rewritten, as briefings tried to portray his move to ITV as money-motivated. He says that he would have been happy to stay at the BBC. He never asked for more money, nor wanted more. He only wanted to carry on doing the programme, *The One Show*, five days a week. And what about Christine?

One of her first thoughts was that Adrian's leaving might be bad news for her too, and when she was summoned to a meeting with her BBC bosses she was quite nervous about it. She met Frank for a soothing coffee and chat beforehand but, as it turned out, there was no need to send the boys round. The BBC was very keen to keep her.

It was widely thought that Chris Hollins would take up the sofa vacancy; he is the son of Chelsea and England half-back (as we used to call them) John Hollins. Chris himself had been a professional footballer and had played first-class cricket at university. He had stood in for Chiles for a week, and had come in through the sports-presenting route. The idea people fastened onto was that Christine would be more of a senior partner than before, although not on a Friday of course, and Hollins, or whoever, would be given time to build up popularity. An insider said 'Christine hoped Adrian would stay, but she is very happy at *The One Show* and her BBC contract is not up for renewal until later this year.'

Food for thought at the BBC: average number of viewers for Adrian and Christine's *One Show* before the news of his leaving was out: 4.3 million. Average number of viewers for *The One Show* when it was presented by substitutes Louise Minchin and Chris Hollins: 4.1 million. Not fair, of course, but numbers mean a lot to senior execs.

On 30 April 2010, Adrian left the BBC. The last *One Show* was a tear-jerker, with the entire *One Show* family there in front of a cheering audience. (Were cheers entirely appropriate? Adrian asked.) Christine began with a review of Adrian's 18 years with the BBC, starting with a youthful, white-shirted fellow with a big, light-brown quiff, talking straight to camera on *Working Lunch*.

On *MOTD2* he was seen testing the friction of the sofa covers with Gordon Strachan, deciding that lack of concentration could lead to their both sliding off onto the floor. Fancy dress towards the end of the season was reflected by Adrian as Batman and, despite everything, as a Wolves supporter. 'There, I've done it,' he said, perhaps thinking that Granddad would be turning in his grave. Previously, it would have been thought more likely that Adrian would swap Christine for Robin and drive the Batmobile to save the good folk of Gotham City, than dress up as a fan of those wanderers of Wolverhampton – unlike Led Zeppelin rocker Robert Plant, who is from West Bromwich and wore Wolves gear as the special guest.

Also as part of the farewell, the West Brom players were doorstepped by a rather unlikely Midlands footie man, Gyles Brandreth, who managed to collect messages of goodwill. Clips were shown from the very first *One Show*, and from a few of the many succeeding ones in which Adrian did something silly. Out of context it was not always clear why he was doing something silly, like dressing as Lion in *The Wizard of Oz*, or having his chest hairs removed by Christine, but it all looked good fun. Whether or not it was intelligent good fun, as previously briefed, we should not like to say, but Adrian and Christine as James Bond types, karate-kicking their way out of trouble from a gang of evil intention, and as Abba, singing 'Take a Chance on Me', were guaranteed to raise a smile. Adrian as Dracula and as a complaining Nancy from *Oliver!* proved why he had been so right to stay away from a career in acting.

There were some touching moments, too, betraying the intimate friendship they had developed, through arm wrestling and snowballing, boxing and fencing, doing the samba, and a tear might even have been shed when Alan Sugar presented the signed photograph of the *One Show* team, and during the big hug at the end.

In advance, the leaders of the UK's three main political parties had recorded tributes and these, much to Adrian's onscreen astonishment, were played during that final appearance as host of *The One Show*.

Gordon Brown was Prime Minister then (it does seem a long time ago). He said, 'Adrian, I think I last had a long talk with you at the Olympics when you did such a marvellous job presenting there, but you've done amazing things on *The One Show* and sports and everything else you've done in reporting, and you've simply done a great job that makes us all proud. And when we talk and meet up, you talk about West Bromwich Albion all the time and I talk about Raith Rovers all the time. At least West Bromwich are going up, I'm afraid Raith Rovers are stuck where they are. But my best wishes to you in everything you do in your future career.'

Conservative leader and future Prime Minister David Cameron said, 'So, Adrian, you're moving on. It's been great appearing on your show, wonderful watching you on *The One Show*. I don't know how they're going to do without you. Best of luck for the future.'

Liberal Democrat leader and future Deputy Prime Minister Nick Clegg summed up the show as well as giving the usual kind of plaudit: 'Adrian, all the best with your move. One of the most unforgettable things I've done since becoming leader of the Liberal Democrats is handling miniature hedgehogs on your *One Show*. You are indelibly etched on my memory for that reason alone.'

At first, Adrian could not believe that the tributes were real. 'I thought they must be lookalikes,' he said. 'I just want to thank all the fantastic *One Show* team for everything, and all of you for watching. I don't know what

I will do without *The One Show* – it has been an absolute ball and honour to work with such great people, most of all Christine obviously, who has just been fantastic.'

As we know and have seen, Adrian and Christine always denied, ridiculed and laughed off any speculation in the media about their being more than just good friends, but anyone watching the last *One Show* could not have doubted the bond between them, the relationship they had developed while presenting the programme, which went beyond any kind of boy-meets-girl attraction and became more like close family.

At the party afterwards at a Hammersmith pub, Adrian was so confident in this truth now being understood that he could refer to it in his speech.

First, he thanked Christine, with whom he'd worked for four years, then Lynne Jones, former deputy editor of *Working Lunch*. He said that he liked to think of his whole career as a sort of Lynne–Christine sandwich.

'That is quite a sandwich and I'm looking forward to making that a reality a little bit later on in the night. Thank you to all of you from Lynne in the first place to the lovely Christine, who's my best friend. I'll miss her desperately, although I'm sure we'll meet for coffee most mornings. In fact we're going for a kebab in my brother's flat tonight.'

The 200 guests at the farewell do included Lord Sugar, Mark Lawrenson, Robert Plant, John Sergeant and the entire *One Show* family. While there had been emotional moments during the actual show, the party was a joyous occasion.

Nobody mentioned the story that had appeared in the *Sun* that morning, which claimed that Adrian wanted

Christine to come with him to ITV. True or not, Christine, for the moment anyway, was marooned on the *One Show* sofa. According to reports, BBC bosses were equally desperate to keep her sitting there, and to find a new Adrian to sit beside her.

The next day, 1 May, a source inside the BBC was confirming what everyone believed in any case: 'There has been interest from ITV for Christine. Last year, she was approached for talks about *This Morning*, and now they are definitely keen on her. Christine has become a star here and there is no way we want her to go. There are various Saturday night shows that are being discussed for her to go solo.'

Blogs and Internet postings on that day comprised the usual rubbish from people with empty spaces instead of lives. Many of them were regular watchers yet professed a delight at Adrian's departure, in which case we have to ask why they spent their half-hours with the show every night. One correspondent clearly had nothing better to do than take time to criticise the political party leaders for having nothing better to do than pay tribute to Adrian. Ah, well. Anyway, among the dross was a sensible and strangely prescient little piece.

> I don't particularly like him but the two of them
> work well together, he will be difficult to replace
> but I am sure they can find someone who will work
> well with Christine Bleakley. I am sure ITV were
> hoping that he would be able to get her to move as
> well because she is more talented and has more
> potential. I suspect that he will find it difficult to fit
> in the more restrictive environment of ITV

breakfast TV and might not last long there.

People might mock The One Show but it is regularly getting large audiences. It might be lightweight some of the time but so were Tonight, Nationwide and Pebble Mill at One. It seems very much in the spirit of these programmes.

According to the *Daily Mirror*, Christine was told she could pick whomsoever she wanted to sit by her right hand. Would it be Paul Merton? Matt Allwright from *Watchdog*? Matthew Wright from Channel Five? Jamie Theakston? Igglepiggle from *In the Night Garden* . . .?

Evans used his Radio 2 show in a rather pre-emptive fashion. 'Not quite the accepted thing to do' seemed to be the general verdict. He boasted that he could get rugby pals Matt Dawson and Austin Healey screen tests to become the co-host on the other four nights with Christine Bleakley. Dawson said that would make him a warm-up act for Evans, but Evans disagreed. The warm-up act would have been 'the other guy', that is Adrian. 'That's what he thought and look what happened to him.'

'This will not go unnoticed,' said one BBC source. 'Chris will have to explain himself. He has to be careful what he says on air, especially when referring to *The One Show*.'

'He shouldn't be criticising Adrian for leaving the BBC,' said another. 'He shouldn't give the impression he has influence on a series he's not been on yet. It's unprofessional. Shades of his boozy days on Radio 1.'

A *One Show* diehard, a colleague of Adrian at the BBC for years, was even more forthright. 'Evans should zip up his mouth. Adrian is leaving as one of the most watched presenters in Britain, while we can't remember when Chris last had a hit TV show. Everyone at the BBC is stressing that Christine Bleakley has the big say on what happens, but Chris seems to think it's him.'

Evans could point to the three months since he took over his Radio 2 slot from Terry Wogan, when he added 1.5 million listeners and broke his predecessor's record for the largest ever audience for a British radio show. And, as he said, 'Who wouldn't want to work with Christine Bleakley?'

He took her to lunch at the Ivy, to discuss their new partnership, after which he said, 'I think what Adrian and Christine have done with the show is fantastic. It's become a much-loved institution in a relatively short space of time and I'm honoured to be able to be joining the team. For me Fridays have always been a little bit special and I want to do my bit to welcome people to the weekend.'

On 23 May 2010, Christine hosted the BAFTA Craft Awards at the Park Lane Hilton. On 24 May, Adrian appeared for the first time on ITV. Before the World Cup, for teeth cutting, there was England against Mexico in a friendly. In the next morning's papers he was generally thought to have been a breath of fresh air, much needed in the too-predictable ITV football studio. Quite so, but it was not like *MOTD2*. The big problem Adrian had to try to overcome was one not of his own making. It was one of the main reasons why the BBC always seems to outdo its commercial rival on football. It can be summed up in one word: adverts.

Quite a few BBC footie men have changed to ITV and been severely discomforted by the commercial break. Adrian, on his first showing, was not discomforted, not in the slightest. When he said, 'Back in just a moment' it was one, two, adverts.

There can't be any ads during the game, naturally, unless Stevie Gerard happens to be scoring a goal at the time, so there has to be a great wodge of them at half-time. The BBC can relax with Gary and the pundits chattering away, replaying key moments at leisure, several times if they want, while ITV has to fit brief comments from the host into a rapid round of other pundits, before the host has to say, 'We'll be right back after the break.' People don't like it and never have. Would they like it any better with the cheery, matey Chiles, Man of the Terraces, trying to hold it together?

Perhaps there was an argument here for doing away with pundits – qualification: used to play football – and leaving the short time entirely to the articulate, witty chap's chap, Adrian. Producers, though, are unwilling to do without pundits, even if they say things like 'Chelsea done today what they do better than any other team' (Alan Shearer).

Back at the BBC, there remained the question of Christine's companion, and not for long was her sofa bereft. With plenty of mention about *The One Show*'s ratings, but no mention, naturally, of the man who had played such a large part in achieving same, the Beeb put out another press release.

Date: 26.05.2010

Category: TV Entertainment; Factual & Arts TV; BBC One

The BBC today confirmed that Jason Manford will

be joining the *One Show* team to present BBC One's popular flagship show alongside Christine Bleakley.

Manford, an award-winning comedian, television and radio presenter, will join the team in July when he will co-host the show with Christine from Monday to Thursday.

Lancashire-born Jason, 29, who is renowned for his cheeky observational humour and friendly approach, says: 'I am thrilled to be part of the *One Show* team. My dad put £10 at 500/1 that I'd get the job so it just made sense.'

Controller of BBC One Jay Hunt says: 'Jason looked instantly at home on the *One Show* sofa. His intelligence and humour strike just the right tone for the programme and he is an exciting addition to the team.'

Like his fellow presenter Chris Evans, Jason has also presented on BBC Radio 2. Last year, he fronted *Jason Manford and Friends*, a two-part series showcasing the cream of the comedy acts from the 2009 Edinburgh Fringe.

The One Show Editor Sandy Smith is thrilled to have Jason on board and adds: 'Jason's strength is his likeability, his natural warmth and his quick wit. He's intelligent and curious about the sort of subjects discussed every day on *The One Show* and is equally at home with the light-hearted and the serious issues.'

Christine and Jason will present the show every Monday to Thursday, with Chris Evans joining Christine every Friday night.

The hugely successful show – which regularly attracts audiences over 5 million viewers – will continue to offer the regular mix of news, current affairs and entertainment alongside some new features and guest slots that will be revealed in the coming weeks.

Notes to Editors

The One Show, which achieved its highest ever ratings this year (7.4 million) and regularly attracts audiences over 5 million, has established itself as essential early evening viewing – combining celebrity guests with topical reports from every corner of the UK.

So. Highest ever ratings this year, when Adrian was on it, before Ginger Knob arrived, and so the obvious thing to do is . . . yes, well. Jason Manford is Man City rather than West Brom, but that shouldn't matter. Best known on TV for *8 out of 10 Cats*, he came to the sofa as an experienced stand-up, and a very good one, too. For example: Manchester weather? It's like Muslims in Iraq. Either Sunni or Shiite.

Alas for Jason, newspaper reports would soon suggest he had been sending explicit Twitter messages to a female fan, asking her to send him topless pictures of herself. By mid November, the kerfuffle would force him to tender his resignation 'to ease the situation surrounding newspaper allegations', allowing him to concentrate on his family and tour commitments.

Speculation continued about Christine's leaving that

sofa just as her new man was landing on it. She split from her agent John Noel. 'There is no doubt that Christine and I will work together again,' said Adrian, although leaving it open as to whether he meant sooner or later. An ITV source said it was an open secret that ITV wanted to pinch her from the Beeb. The BBC was rumoured to be unable to match the suggested money that ITV was alleged to have offered her, but instead had apparently promised to make her the biggest female star on television.

Quite how the size of one's starship is measured if not in spondulicks we cannot be certain. Perhaps it is calculated according to the number of paparazzi on the pavement outside one's house, or in the number of secret long-lens photographs taken of one while on the holiday beach. If so, that seems to be scant consolation for the lack of sponds.

She wasn't going, anyway. Soon after Adrian said they would work together one day, Christine supposedly agreed a new contract and gave her blessing to her new co-presenter.

'I don't want to go anywhere,' said Christine. 'I love Jason. I've met him a few times and our rapport is getting better all the time. I love funny men, guys who don't take themselves too seriously. The first time I met him, we were interviewing him on the show and he was dressed as the Tin Man. You can't not like that, can you? He will be brilliant. I'm confident our chemistry will be as good as the one Adrian and I shared. We just need time.'

A BBC insider (yes, it's him again, or her) said, 'Christine does not want a megabucks, golden handcuffs deal as she does not want the pressure that comes with it.

She is hugely popular within the BBC and we have absolute faith in her.'

'Seven million viewers is a phenomenal amount for a magazine programme,' said a BBC source. 'People warmed to Christine immediately. There's no doubt that she's a valuable asset. She is hugely important to the BBC.'

Opinion was divided. On the one hand, Christine was recognised as being naturally inclined to loyalty, realising that she was where she was because of the confidence shown in her by her original BBC managers in Belfast. On the other hand, she was clearly a clever lass. With Adrian gone, her own value to the BBC had increased and she would have been a fool not to make the most of the opportunity thus presented to her.

All sorts of shows, from *Countryfile* to *Olympics 2012* and back again to *Strictly*, were said to have been offered to Christine. Would she stay or would she go? By 8 June, the *Daily Mail* was reporting that a £2 million deal would keep her at the BBC. Also on that day, Christine was awarded Presenter of the Year by *Glamour* magazine. On 9 June, the *Daily Star* was saying there would be no £2 million deal.

And from the letters page of the *Daily Mail*: 'I can't understand the popularity of the woman on *The One Show* on BBC1 each evening. Her accent is almost indecipherable. Lord Reith must be turning in his grave. Jonathan M Balcon, Tunbridge Wells, Kent.'

So there really is a 'Disgusted of Tunbridge Wells', and he reads the *Daily Mail*. There's a surprise. He should know that the almost indecipherable accent was much mellowed from its original state by this time.

Let us leave the last word on this factual reporting of rumours to the *Guardian* and the *Daily Mirror*: 'Christine Bleakley is poised to sign a two-year deal understood to be worth about £1m to stay at the BBC to front *The One Show*, host a new Saturday night programme and play a part in the coverage of the 2012 Olympics. Bleakley is not thought to have signed the new deal.' And, 'She told the *Daily Mirror* today that she is "so happy here [at the BBC] I'm staying put, absolutely".'

The new deal, which would run until September 2012, would see her pay bumped up by more than £100,000 a year. In addition, she was understood to have been offered a role in the BBC's London 2012 Olympics coverage, although she would not be 'the face', as had been previously reported. BBC executives were also keen for her to host a new Saturday night show.

'Christine is a great talent and she is currently under contract at the BBC. There is nothing more we can say at this stage,' said a spokesman, saying nothing more. 'We look forward to talking to her about future projects in due course.'

In the *Daily Express*, Richard and Judy congratulated Christine on her decision to stay, not for any reason to do with ITV or Adrian, but because of the early-morning starts the move would have entailed. 'It was bad enough when we were hosting *This Morning* in Liverpool and commuting from Manchester, setting our daily alarm for 5am. Breakfast telly is even rougher on the constitution with its 3.30am calls. Insomnia, digestion problems, dead-looking skin and chronic fatigue afflict almost everyone involved.'

Meanwhile, Irish comedian Dara Ó Briain was selected

to replace Adrian on *The Apprentice: You're Fired!* and Colin Murray, also, like Christine, from Belfast, would do *MOTD2*. And that wasn't the last word on the speculation after all. Christine signed with agents Avalon Management, who also represented Adrian, and issued a statement:

> In the light of constant speculation about my future I'd like to clarify a few things. It's been reported that I've signed for ITV, signed for the BBC and in both cases for astronomical sums. The truth is that as it stands, my current contract with the BBC ends shortly. I'm flattered to have received great offers from both the BBC and ITV, which I now have to decide between. I am torn.
>
> On one hand I am really keen to work again with Adrian. We have a brilliant relationship on and off screen, although I can't say I'd particularly relish the idea of dealing with him at 5am every morning. On the other hand the BBC is incredibly good to me and I'm very close to everyone on *The One Show*, which I love presenting. The BBC's plans for *The One Show* are very exciting. I expect to make a decision on my future very soon.

At the same time, the BBC was embroiled in a row over pay for those many staff who did not appear on screen. The offer was deemed to be poor.

The National Union of Journalists general secretary, Jeremy Dear, said, 'We appreciate the BBC is trying to cut the cake to help the lowest paid but it is unacceptable that a third of journalists would receive no pay rise and that for the third year running BBC staff are being offered a deal which is significantly below inflation and significantly below the rise in the licence fee. Quite simply, the cake isn't big enough.'

If that was one of Nigella's cakes, surely it would be big enough, and there would be rises all round. Not so. In an email to all staff sent over the weekend, the head of BBC People, Lucy Adams, wrote, 'The pay offer will benefit almost 70 per cent of our staff and our aim has been to direct the available funds to those staff who earn the least.'

There was no choice. We had to find out what an insider thought. 'In the week when we can find a million quid to try and keep Christine Bleakley on *The One Show*, it calls into question senior management's understanding of what licence fee payers believe represents value for money.'

Back at ITV, the football World Cup was coming up and the hero of *MOTD2*, Olympics 2008, Euro 2008 and so on, Adrian, had to be the man for the job. Everyone has forgotten that time on the previous World Cup, when Adrian had been BBC to the core and had taken such delight in telling his BBC viewers that Serbia and Ivory Coast now had a dead rubber to play. 'Full coverage of that over on ITV,' he had said with a little smile.

When the World Cup did come around, Adrian had just taken a holiday and had a car smash. 'We were in Slovenia, driving to Croatia. A girl just came around the corner and slammed her car into the side of us, in a hired Lexus. The police turned up and just stared at me and my mates, and then at this traumatised Slovenian girl. You could see what they were thinking, but we had a West

Brom shirt with us. We showed it to the coppers and said "Robert Koren plays for us!" and they waved us away. They love Koren in Slovenia. Funny thing was, he was released by West Brom the next day, but we were out of Slovenia by then.'

After the World Cup farce of 2006, England manager Fabio Capello banned the WAGs from the players' hotel, but there was nothing to stop a few of them going to the matches. How could TV cameramen and vision mixers resist a cutaway to a lovely WAG when her husband/boyfriend/significant other scored a goal or was felled by a crunching tackle? Christine had now acquired super-WAG status, and surely her Frank would score (he didn't – the one he got was disallowed).

Adrian wasn't far into his World Cup before one of his greatest fans was on the blog. This is one of those self-obsessed bloggers who imagine that somebody cares what they think, and that the act of typing a few words into outer space makes them somehow centres of attention. Here's what he put, re Germany versus Australia:

I hate to sound obsessed but Adrian Chiles really is the pits and his God awful presenting made the build up to this game a complete chore. Nobody gives a flying duck how much the English hate the Germans and the Australians and his introductions are increasingly straying into very tasteless xenophobia. He also needs to accept that he is not funny and thus needs to drop his constant hesitant attempts at comedy. Good God, where's Steve Ryder when you need him?

This is the same fellow who, more than three years earlier, wrote this:

> Turning to things closer to home I nearly laughed my leg off when I heard that Adrian Chiles was sent used arsewipes in the post. Finally, somebody else who agrees with me that he is a load of old crap (and no, I didn't send them before anybody asks). Happen somebody picked up on my previously mentioned idea that he rather resembles Arseface and the rest of the gag made itself.

There's self-delusion for you. 'I didn't send them before anybody asks'? As if anybody would ask. 'Happen somebody picked up on my . . . idea'? His idea? This man needs help. Perhaps somebody could pick him up and take him to a quiet room and force him to read other people's blogs all day long.

As Adrian left the BBC, other old favourites were breathing their last. A BBC statement said:

> The size of the *Working Lunch* audience has suffered a slow but steady decline since 2001. A re-launch of *Working Lunch* in October 2008 has failed to reverse the audience decline which now appears to be stable. It's always sad when a programme reaches the end of its life cycle, but our business coverage has never been about one programme.

Working Lunch as we know began in 1994 with Adrian Chiles and Adam Shaw.

Chiles [the statement continued], who announced
last week that he was quitting the BBC, left
Working Lunch in 2007 to work on BBC One
teatime programme *The One Show* on a full-time
basis. *Working Lunch* has recently been attracting
an audience of around 300,000 viewers.

Among that 300,000 used to be somebody very similar to
Disgusted of Tunbridge Wells. If anyone ever aspires to be
a television executive, bear in mind that – whatever you
do – you will get some of this:

Over the years I have watched with increasing
despondency, the quality of the BBC's niche
programmes deteriorate. Programmes about cars,
computers, home improvement and science &
technology have all been progressively dumbed
down in an attempt to attract a wider audience,
completely ignoring the fact that the core audience
for these programmes, who were actually interested
in the subject, had drifted away as these
programmes metamorphosed into themed light
entertainment.

I have, up until now, tolerated this gradual
erosion of quality with a sense of resignation, but
your wilful vandalism against Working Lunch is
just too much to tolerate. Your coverage of business
and finance is already extremely thin, and to allow
TV entropy to corrode one of your very few
programmes aimed at those who are both interested
in finance and averagely intelligent is unforgivable.

The set looks like something from Strictly Come

Dancing, the introduction spoken over what passes for music and the two presenters speaking alternate lines are gimmicks that lost their novelty years ago. In addition, having a presenter who is dressed as if she is going to a party, and another casually dressed as if for gardening are not appropriate to a serious business and finance programme. It is also discourteous to the majority of your guests, who are business people and dress accordingly, to be interviewed by people whose dress code, rightly or wrongly, conveys disrespect.

As a public service broadcaster, whose income is guaranteed, you have an obligation to produce a reasonable number of serious programmes on important subjects. You do not have a mandate to sacrifice these programmes in an indiscriminate attempt to chase ratings, which is the function of the commercial broadcasters.

Wow. Well, clearly this is some reviewer. Not only does he/she know what the sets of *Strictly* look like, but can also drop in words like 'entropy' (the name given to one of the quantitative elements that determine the thermodynamic condition of a portion of matter – *Shorter Oxford Dictionary*). Hmm. Maybe what was meant was atrophy – wasting away. We'd prefer an entrecôte anyway.

Other contributors to the general alarm over *Working Lunch* were saying the same thing but in a slightly different way:

Working Lunch used to be fun with Adrian and

Adam. Even after Adrian left, Adam and the team kept it a pleasant lunchtime programme. Y'see they had a sense of humour AND were credible.

Working Lunch used to be such a good programme – especially when Adrian was on it. Now utter rubbish. Have stopped watching. Thank goodness we now have Sky.

CHAPTER NINE

DAYBREAK

The press now suggested that Christine had dillied and dallied, dallied and dillied, lost her way, and was hoping to manipulate the BBC into making her a better deal. She denied this absolutely. She had a contract until the October, so there had been no rush to renegotiate, and then suddenly up came the ginger thing, and off went Adrian.

'Everything I knew and loved changed overnight,' she said. Over the years of *The One Show*, Christine and Adrian had become an onscreen item. They were the Mixed Doubles champions. Take one of the partners away and ask the other, 'What next?' and you just might get the answer, 'Well, hang on a minute, I'm not sure yet.' Ask again, 'Will it be the same thing with a different partner, or a different thing with the same partner?' and you still might not get a firm reply straightaway.

Christine had worked for the BBC for 14 of her 31 years. Even when she got the call from ITV, it was still a massive decision. There had, after all, been a lot of serendipity at *The One Show*. Adrian had been going fine with Myleene Klass, whose leaving resulted in a shortlist of eight girls for her job, and Christine was not top of that list to start with, but she rose to the top and stayed there. So, if Adrian's new doubles partner in the new ball game was not to be Christine, who would it be? Would there have to be another shortlist, and another selection by a mixture of luck and judgement, or would the known and understood triple-X factor be the preferred option?

Adrian was sure. 'At all costs I felt we had to be together again.' And that was purely for TV-professional reasons, and nothing to do with feeling gutted over the way he had, as he saw it, been forced out of the Beeb. 'It was an awful, awful business,' he said. 'We were both very happy to stay, and nothing needed to change. But obviously change was suggested on *The One Show* I couldn't live with and that's why I left. We were both criticised for the way we conducted ourselves, but it was such a long, stressful time. Our livelihoods were on the line, and something that was very precious to us both – *The One Show* – had been basically taken away from us to a lesser or greater extent.'

Christine added, 'Suddenly lots of people wanted to talk and I was always brought up to think silence is golden and there's a dignity in keeping your mouth shut about certain things, but at that stage I was being hurried into making a big decision. Ultimately no one's died, this is not life or death, but I missed working with Adrian.'

Christine's promise to decide very soon did not come soon enough for the BBC, which lost patience and, one Sunday afternoon when everybody else was in the pub, walking in the woods or snoozing in the armchair, withdrew the £450,000-a-year offer.

'Christine is still unable to make a decision and therefore we have regretfully withdrawn our offer as we have to put the interests of *The One Show* audience first and the current uncertainty does not allow us to do that.'

Jana Bennett, BBC director of vision, added, 'How long to wait for a decision to be made is part of my job. At some point negotiations have to come to an end. We had been open to continuing discussions up to a point, but to leave it too long would have meant not knowing what we were going to be doing.'

Within two hours of that statement being issued by the BBC, ITV issued its own statement saying Christine had signed an exclusive three-year deal. This was taken to mean that there would be a new GMTV breakfast show after September, when her BBC contract finished, on which she would be reunited with Adrian.

In an echo of the trade unions' objections to big money for stars, MPs also had been putting in their two penn'orth. Should the BBC spend so much money on one person, when the public sector at large is being asked to tighten belts, breathe in, and generally have a smaller slice of the aforementioned cake?

John Whittingdale, chairman of House of Commons Media Select Committee, said, 'This is public money. If she feels she can go and earn vast sums in the private sector, then good luck to her.'

The BBC said it had been discussing terms with Christine, based on her expressed wish to be a player in the re-launch of *The One Show*. There had been confidence too that she would be more attracted by career developments on her own account, rather than being the Wise to Adrian's Morecambe. She would have been Number One on *The One Show* and would have had everything else she wanted, apart from the peak-time Saturday night show she was said to have been asking for.

'With that in mind, we made a full and final offer to her several weeks ago and made it clear we would not be entering into a bidding war with other channels.'

A BBC source, clearly in imaginative mood and perhaps hoping for a job on Radio 4, said 'It's as if the BBC was a boy who asked her to the prom, and she wouldn't say yes because she hoped the high school jock would ask her instead.'

It was common knowledge that the BBC offer had been worth £900,000 over two years, while the ITV contract was said to be for £6 million, or £4 million, over three years.

Christine once again issued a statement.

I am looking forward to a brand-new experience at ITV albeit with an old friend. And it will be exciting to work alongside Peter Fincham again who kindly gave me a break on *The One Show* in the first place. I have had the most wonderful three years at the BBC and *The One Show*. It has consumed my life and I would not have had it any other way; I have made great friends and met some incredible people.

I have been torn between working with Adrian Chiles and remaining at the BBC. I fully understand the BBC had to move more swiftly than I could, and as a result they've managed to help make my mind up for me. The BBC, and specifically Jay Hunt and her team, have been nothing but supportive, fair and encouraging since I stepped foot inside there.

Everywhere there is jam to be had, or people are enjoying a picnic, you'll generally find a wasp, and wasps don't come much sharper than a pack of bloggers called the Watch With Mothers – 'We watch television so you don't have to.' One blogger, giving her name as 'Justrestingmyeyes', is clearly a witty and clever writer, and possibly might be wasting her talents. We quote her in full, in the sure and certain hope that her views represent those of a large mass of British intellectuals, thus:

The BBC's inexplicably popular, obscure nature-poking/local-injustice borefest *The One Show* is falling apart at its comfy teatime sofa seams. First Adrian Chiles jumped ship after taking exception to Chris Evan's [*sic*] being helicoptered in to spread his smug charms and mid-'90s catchphrases on the Friday edition of the show.

Now Christine Bleakley, the ship's beautiful pouting wooden figurehead, has wrenched herself free and is floating gracefully after Chiles' frantically doggy-paddling form, both bound for the desolate island of ITV.

Chiles is already installed as chief-thrower-to-ads on ITV's World Cup coverage and will shortly be taking over the intellectual powerhouse that is GMTV. It seems natural that Bleakley will join him on the early morning sofa to recreate the chemistry they beamed over our spag bols every day. But would it be willingly?

According to Digital Spy the BBC has been chucking the toys (that it's only just picked up after the whole Chiles kerfuffle) straight out of the pram again:

'We made a full and final offer to her several weeks ago and made it clear we would not be entering into a bidding war with other channels.

'Christine is still unable to make a decision and therefore we have regretfully withdrawn our offer as we have to put the interests of *The One Show* audience first and the current uncertainty does not allow us to do that.'

Handbags! Nose-cutting for face-spiteing! Taking ball and going home behaviour!

Incredible bravery (or possible stupidity) from Auntie Beeb there. And good news for ITV, who now have an embarrassment of talent-riches after running a channel for years on the ground-up bones of Ant'n'Dec and the plentiful tears of Vernon Kay.

So now attention turns to who will be the fragrant Bleakley's replacement next to unproven new host Jason Manford. We've got a few ideas up our ragged sleeves:

BBC Breakfast Newsreader Autobot 3000: By which we mean Kate Silverton, Susannah Reid, or one of the many other interchangeable ice queens who are the perfect news/lifestyle presenting combination of autocue reading skills, lipgloss and interior deadness. If only we could get over the feeling that they will one day be activated by a malevolent alien force and will gaze through the camera and kill us all with laser beams from their eyes.

Carol Thatcher: A leftfield choice, but this could be her rehabilitation into our cold, unfeeling hearts. As long as she doesn't turn up in blackface for at least the first few weeks, she'll get on fine.

James Corden: Frankly, at his current rate of exposure, it just seems bleakly inevitable. Bleakly! Do you see what we have done did there? What, you could do better? We know, we know. Course you could.

Over to you, WWMers: who should park their perky buttocks next to Manford in the neon One Show mothership?

Despite the BBC saying that everybody had the right to do whatever they liked, it did look a little as if the corporation had made a boob. Way back in August 2008, at the Edinburgh International Television Festival, Jay Hunt had told of plans to use Chris Evans as a fill-in for Adrian on holidays. The response of Adrian and Christine had been, it appeared, to make sure they took very few holidays, and the ones they did take were in such a way as to make sure Evans didn't get a look-in. Nor did he. Then, come November 2009, it was Evans again as Ms Hunt pushed him forward for a new, all-singing, all-dancing edition of *The One Show* on a Friday, signing him up before consulting Adrian, and letting the news out while Adrian was away on holiday.

Entirely predictably to everyone except senior BBC

execs, this upset Adrian no end, and put in chain the series of events that led to both his and Christine's leaving. And, to top it all, the BBC announced the withdrawal of its offer to Christine, knowing perfectly well that she hadn't signed yet with ITV and so might be out of a job entirely.

BBC creative director Alan Yentob went on Radio 5 Live to put his case: 'Having all these negotiations in the public eye in this way clearly was not helpful. We decided she'd had a very long time to say yes and if she couldn't make her mind up she didn't want to come. If you're negotiating with someone else as well you feel a bit of a patsy if you're sitting down, so we stopped and said, "Do you want to come?" and we didn't hear, so we felt that was the right decision. People were waiting, including Chris Evans, talented people . . . and in the end the most important thing was her commitment.'

There was a point here. The BBC has always been known for growing its own talent, with one or two exceptions such as Graham Norton. Adrian and Christine were classical cases, coming from nowhere, being nurtured, gradually being given more exposure and then, like others before them, being tempted to the Other Side by the big bucks. If Mr Yentob was familiar with the Marriott Edgar story of 'The Lion and Albert', he might have remembered the last verse.

> At that Mother got proper blazing.
> 'And thank you, sir, kindly,' said she.
> 'What, waste all our lives raising children
> To feed ruddy Lions? Not me!'

Alas for Mr Yentob and the BBC, feeding the ruddy lions at ITV seems to be part of the job description. Still, a replacement for Christine had to be found, and that would have to be from within the ranks. According to the *Sun*, ten women were auditioned on the sofa with Jason Manford, including Sky newsreader Charlotte Hawkins (Sky? some mistake surely), Liz Bonnin from the BBC1 show *Bang Goes the Theory*, Melanie Sykes (she was the cream of Manchester, the girl in the Boddington's ads), the news-oriented Kate Silverton and sport-oriented Gabby Logan. 'Adrian and Christine were not big names when they started. It's vital that she (the new presenter) has the chemistry with Jason,' said the Beeb.

In fact, they did a Christine, Welsh version, and selected a relatively unknown presenter, Alex Jones, a 32-year-old from Cardiff, to join Jason Manford in a presenting team that wouldn't cost a fortune in salaries. In a curious and rapid change of fortune, Christine had picked and lobbied for Jason to join her, after they met at a Channel 4 party. Now Jason was suddenly being asked to pick his new Christine. It was a process he likened to speed dating.

Miss Jones had been on Welsh TV for 10 years or so but was largely unheard of outside Wales. She comes from Ammanford, Carmarthenshire, where she went to a Welsh-speaking school. She trained as a ballet dancer before studying film and TV at Aberystwyth University, then worked as a TV researcher but not a very good one, she says. 'I was really forgetful and dippy and I think I was too young for the responsibility.'

Once in front of the camera in Wales, Alex had blossomed, with Welsh-language successes and coverage of Six Nations rugby with Jonathan Davies.

'I'm absolutely thrilled to bits to be joining *The One Show*. I watch it at home every night on my sofa and can't believe I'm now swapping it for the *One Show* sofa! It is the break I have only ever dreamed of and can't believe I'm getting to work with Jason Manford, who I think is just fantastic – it is the icing on the cake.'

More cake, look you. BBC's daytime controller, Liam Keelan, said, 'I'm delighted to welcome Alex to the *One Show* team. Her screen test with Jason was outstanding and from that moment we knew she was the one.'

No mention anywhere that she just happened to look exactly like Christine, except possibly (according to certain eagle-eyed viewers) slightly more prominent in what Terry Wogan used to call the chestal area. Alex said, 'People say I look like Christine. Well, at least they don't say I look like Adrian Chiles. Christine is a beautiful girl, but really the similarity ends after the fact that we both have brunette hair.' Really? Can we mention teeth?

Anyway, the BBC would be saving on icing and cake compared with what they'd have been paying her predecessor.

Both new presenters were nervous of following such a brilliant double act, but they weren't going to change much. 'It's more us getting used to the show rather than us changing it,' said Alex. 'It's going to be tough because they were great on screen and engaged me as a viewer. I think we'll be different, a bit more brotherly and sisterly, but if we're half as good as they were we'll be pleased.'

Although ignored by snobby critics, *The One Show* had become a national treasure. 'The trick is it doesn't take itself too seriously,' Jason Manford has said. 'Everyone knows it's a mad show, no one thinks it's

Question Time. It's jovial to have it on in the background when you're having your tea. It's a fun half-hour before the depressing soaps are on.'

This is what Lucy Mangan thought about their debut:

Chiles and Bleakley brought what you might term a
professional amateurism to proceedings – they
made it look easy, natural, like they'd just suddenly
found themselves on a sofa surrounded by cameras
and kept on chatting about things they thought
might amuse while our tea went down. Manford
and Jones could be Chiles and Bleakley's
doppelgängers – inoffensively dough-faced
Everyman on the left, attractive olive-skinned
brunette with piano keyboard smile on the right.
Something for everyone to relate, aspire and warm
to still. May I be the first to say that Jones's hair is
so glossily fantastic that it really should have been
given separate billing.

At first, the general view was that Alex needed some time to settle in, but she would get there in the end. The show, created out of the relationship on screen of Adrian and Christine, and wished good luck by them in a special note, looked to be safe in new hands. Coincidentally, the new team made their debut on the date, 16 August, that Christine had first joined Adrian three years before. The difference was the extra millions of viewers built up in those three years.

Meanwhile, it became clear that the GMTV name would disappear. Among the new names being talked about was ITV Breakfast. Whatever it would be called,

ITV boss Alison Sharman was sure there needed to be a sea change. 'Based on the feedback we have gained from viewer research and from the listening groups, almost universally, the need for a new look and feel to the programme is paramount. Included in this is an opportunity for a new name.'

A comment by the *Guardian*'s Media Monkey suggested that matters might go further than a mere name:

> ITV's plans for *This Morning*-linked merchandising imply similar branding spin-offs for GMTV once the breakfast show is revamped in the autumn. Obvious possibilities include the Adrian Chiles pram, bulging with throwable toys, and the Christine Bleakley 'I'm so not a WAG' fashion range, made up of daywear and swimwear that sharply differentiate you from the horde of sunbed-blasted blondes.

Of course, after all the hoo-ha, it would have been astonishing if the media pundits did not wonder if it would all turn out nice again. The BBC's rather unusual step of withdrawing Christine's offer on a Sunday afternoon had not had any negative effect, if any had been desired, because she had been signed to ITV by the evening. Still, not a great start.

Nevertheless, Peter McHugh, a long-time GMTV director, thought that things were looking up. 'It's a good move, very good news for ITV. The public see them as a double act. It also solves the problem of who they would have to find, to pair him with.'

The new ITV1 breakfast programme was scheduled to start on Monday, 6 September. After 17 years, the *GMTV* structure of separate pieces was to be demolished in favour of a show with a single thread of identity. The aim would be, it was supposed, to make the new programme fit better with the rest of ITV1. There would be new sets, new everything, but the big question was, would Adrian and Christine transfer their magic from a half-hour evening show to a three-hour show starting with the dawn?

Adrian, the pundits pointed out, was closely linked with football and the blokey kind of audience that sport mostly attracted. *The One Show* had been big with the top half of the age range, whereas morning ITV was chiefly for younger mums. Christine would be all right, wouldn't she? She was a kind of role model for all the yummy mummies, without being one herself. But that glum old self-deprecating Adrian, at home and happiest moaning about West Brom in the public bar, could he be the chirpy, good-morning-sunshine type that viewers wanted while burning their toast? The ads on ITV mornings were generally for household stuff, toys, food, medicine, not what you normally expected on the hoardings around a football pitch. Advertisers saw the target audience as the one they most wanted to reach if they were selling consumer goods.

Doubts also were expressed because of the high expectations accompanying the pair. Could Christine live up to it all, or was *The One Show* really the peak of her career? Was she jumping ship, or walking the plank? ITV can be tough. Auntie BBC was the more caring place, wasn't it? What would happen to Christine if it all went wrong? Adrian would still have his football, probably, but would she have somewhere to go? Maybe, some cynics suggested, she was canny enough to know all that and was happy with her own millions and those of Mr Lampard, were she to become 'er indoors.

The paps certainly thought that everything about her and the Chelsea footballer was worth a picture. We can only wonder at the definition of news as seen by, for example, the *Daily Mail*:

> She's on our screens every single weekday, so you would think Christine Bleakley would know how to maintain her modesty in front of a camera. But the 31-year-old presenter made a schoolgirl fashion error while out on a coffee run with boyfriend Frank Lampard yesterday, as she teamed her sheer black top with a white bra. Under the photographers' flashlights, the top was turned see-through, displaying her uncoordinated underwear underneath.

Well, well, well! Now there's a funny thing. Fancy having underwear underneath. Add two pictures of Christine carrying take-out coffee and one of Frank with some carrier bags and, wow, you have a story.

Vanessa Feltz in the *Daily Express* implied that there was not much to Christine, apart from her looks and engaging smile. Certainly, said the stunning Vanessa, Christine was 'no supersonic combination of Esther Rantzen, Carol Vorderman and Barbara Walters' (why wasn't V. Feltz in that list?). Indeed, La Bleakley's greatest talent was for making Adrian Chiles look good, so was that worth £4 million? Ms Feltz wanted to know.

Despite extensive research, we have been unable to find anyone who wants to know what Vanessa is worth.

There was also the ratings situation. *BBC Breakfast* had overtaken *GMTV* three years before and was running further away. The BBC now pulled in an average of 1.5 million viewers, a 34 per cent share of a smallish market, since most people listen to the radio in the morning rather than watch telly. At the peak, towards eight o'clock, BBC could have 2 million while *GMTV* had 1.1 million with an average of 800,000. These numbers are very small beer compared with radio, which is also much cheaper. Two bloggers explain:

> Am I alone in finding many presenters thoroughly unappealing? I avoid any programme where the presenter is apparently more important than the people interviewed or discussed. Jonathan Ross is one example. [. . .]

> If I need updating over breakfast I choose either to listen on the radio or read, in hard copy or online. I have never seen why I would want to have breakfast tv on. On those rare occasions where some other member of the family decides otherwise the trainwreck inanity of it results in it being turned off, unless that family member has not gone to bed yet and thus is not in their right mind. Brain candy, and as good for your brain as candy is for your teeth.

While all this was going on, England's World Cup was dribbling towards its shameful end. Martin Kelner had been given the job of hosting the giant-screen showings in Leeds's Millennium Square, and had become fascinated by the crowd's reactions to the giant-size non-footballers, the presenters and experts, as they appeared before their well-oiled audience many, many miles away.

> Giant Adrian Chiles, I have noticed over the tournament, has been greeted with particular, not venom exactly, but definitely disrespect, as a knot of the more forthright critics began a chant relating to a solitary sexual pursuit. I am assuming this kind of abuse is an inevitable consequence of recent publicity, reports of his salary, and the fact he used to share a sofa with Christine Bleakley. Giant Gary Lineker, interestingly, provoked a more muted reaction, despite the crisp commercials, the young wife, and probably being far better rewarded than Chiles, which shows what a fickle beast La Foule, as Edith Piaf called it, can be.

And Christine came home on the England team aircraft, but not as a journalist. Maybe one day we'll find out what was said on that funereal trip.

And then the news was out. ITV would drop the name *GMTV* from its breakfast programme, rebranding it as *Daybreak*, with new presenters Adrian Chiles and Christine Bleakley. So what would happen to the old presenters?

Lorraine Kelly's show, *GMTV with Lorraine*, which ran for 25 minutes after 9am, would be renamed *Lorraine* and would be the 'home of celebrity interviews and inspirational stories from exceptional people'.

GMTV presenter Penny Smith had already left and Ben Shephard and Andrew Castle would be going before the autumn re-launch.

Christine had been with the BBC since she was 17. Adrian joined a bit later but, apart from a few false starts, had been a BBC person for the whole of his working life. Confident professionals that they are, there was bound to be a certain amount of trepidation, especially when we see the expectations they had to meet. This is a press release from ITV.

Providing viewers with a fantastic launch to the ITV day, *DAYBREAK* will come from brand new, state-of-the-art studios and forms a key part of ITV's ongoing strategy to renew and refresh its programming.

Joining anchors Adrian and Christine will be an unrivalled team of special correspondents tasked with setting the day's agenda; delivering reputation building news and distinctive, credible journalism; engaging entertainment content, major exclusive interviews; as well as eye-catching consumer items, plus health, sport, human interest and lifestyle features.

Director of Factual, Daytime and GMTV, Alison Sharman said:

'*DAYBREAK* plays a key part in ITV's ongoing transformation and reflects the fact that creative renewal lies at the heart of our schedule, which is being modernised and improved under Peter Fincham.

'Since acquiring GMTV we have carried out a

thorough review and set out to transform and significantly invest in a business that had been lagging behind its competitors in recent years. Change, both on and off screen, is an essential part of the process in our bid to reclaim the top breakfast show spot.

'We want to ensure that the core audience of housewives with children keep watching but are also determined to attract new viewers to our revitalised breakfast show.

'As we approach the next stage of this transformational journey our newly confirmed anchors – Christine and Adrian – will be the lynchpins of *DAYBREAK* with their unique and brilliant partnership.'

So, as lynchpins (or linchpins, if you prefer the more usual spelling), the unique and brilliant Christine and Adrian were briefed to keep the wheels on during a transformational journey, and that's no easy matter. More instructions included being authoritative but not dull, not looking glum, having fun, laughing in the right places, and being credible, classy and very high-quality. Compared with the predecessor programme *GMTV*, for example, competitions were to be less cheesy and guests more interesting. Possibly these last details had not been fully absorbed by the time of the first show, when competitive viewers were asked how many years there are in a century, there were noncompetitive interviews with the parents of babies whose birth coincided with the launch of *Daybreak*, and one of the video guests was not a duck but a dog on a skateboard.

Chiles on *Daybreak*: 'An awful lot of thought, time and money has gone into developing *Daybreak*. Now, if Christine and I can get our words out in the right order at that time in the morning, there's every chance we can help make it a big success.'

Bleakley: '*Daybreak* is a brand-new experience for me. All the elements are in place, Adrian and I just have to make sure we can put them in order. Not sure if I relish 3am wake-up calls but I am sure Adrian's jolly demeanour will make it all the more enjoyable. I'm really excited and I can't wait to get started.'

A few days before day broke, Adrian was anchoring the England game against Bulgaria, 3 September 2010. One critic, Martin Kelner of the *Guardian*, wrote that the ads were more interesting than the 'uncomfortably stilted badinage' between Chiles and his new set of pundits, and likened him to a hostage being forced by kidnappers to make a video pleading for ransom money.

> I do not know what has happened to Chiles. Without being funny himself, at his best, on programmes such as *The Apprentice: You're Fired!*, he engendered an atmosphere of good humour through his ease with live television – not a skill to be undervalued – and a certain bluff geniality. On Friday, all that seemed to have disappeared.

Well, Martin, it was Adrian's ease with live television that landed him his new life with ITV, with accompanying razzmatazz from the media. If he appeared to be slightly less than his usual relaxed self, perhaps we can ask Mr Kelner what he would feel like if he were suddenly asked to write leaders for *The Times* rather than a TV review on the back page of the sports section. 'The host,' said Kelner, 'ploughed his usual West Brom furrow: "We're rubbish, us, but we'll support us till we die, because that's the kind of wacky folk we are. Back with more after the break." '

There's no pleasing some people, but we can be sure, as time passes, that any resemblance between Adrian Chiles and a kidnap-victim video will disappear entirely.

On the day before the great day broke, Barbara Ellen of the *Observer* wrote that she:

> couldn't care less about their chemistry. Nor do I have any animosity towards Chiles or Bleakley, though one can see why some might have become irritated. What a huge smarmy luvvie fuss they made of all of this. Conjoined twins could have been successfully separated with less drama than these two, um, leaving one television channel for another.
>
> Certainly, they have played a blinder, going from quite-liked screen couple to greedy, overpaid, overrated idiots everyone hates, within just a few short months. Jonathan Ross will be furious – it took him years to achieve that.

Everyone hates? Presumably these are the same everyones who, in the media, made all the drama. The huge, smarmy, luvvie fuss was hyped up by a fascinated collection of journalists and commentators who felt obliged, first of all, to cover the great swap-over and then, once sufficient smoke had been generated, fire their spiteful bullets from positions of safety.

Adrian and Christine's first morning on *Daybreak* was a little nervous, too, which was hardly surprising. Christine had trouble with her skirt. Chiles on their studio: 'It's extremely big. I've worked in some right little shoe cupboards in my time. The view is simply magnificent. For example, I get my timings from the clock on top of the Shell tower over there. If we move round, we can see St Paul's. They've got to get those cranes out of the way – can somebody have a word, please? They're spoiling the view slightly. Then, there's the Gherkin, and finally the Oxo tower. Other stock cubes are available but that is the Oxo tower. I don't know what else you can say about it.'

When Adrian walked across the studio to sports maestro Dan Lobb, he said, 'See how smoothly I did this. It's going terribly well: I haven't tripped up the stairs or anything.'

They discussed the women's rugby World Cup. Adrian revealed that he had always watched the women's rugby with special interest, 'because a girl I used to play kiss-chase with in the playground went on to play second row for England. I won't name her, because last time I did she went nuts. I think escaping me in kiss-chase is where she got her fitness from.'

Later, instead of Gyles Brandreth to talk to, they had Tony Blair, who had just caused a riot in Dublin with his book-signing. Actually, Blair and Chiles were old colleagues. They had co-presented an edition of the football phone-in, *6-0-6*, on Radio 5 Live back in 2006, with the World Cup being played out in Germany.

'What's the point?' asked Adrian, of the signings. 'The book's flying off the shelves, anyway.' Possibly he was hoping the former Prime Minister was going to confess, saying that it was his duty to ensure that everyone in the known world had the opportunity to get his autograph, but no. Slightly off guard, Blair said he was seriously thinking about it, but what a pity it was that a tiny minority should disturb the due process of things. Later, he cancelled his London signings.

Chiles's opening words for the much-heralded programme did not bear the marks of forethought. 'Dawn is happening, day is breaking here behind us. We spent good money bringing this view to you so I'm glad you can see it.'

Daybreak did not get off to a good start from some critics' points of view, either. The TV folk 'seem to have modelled their set on the lobby of a Premier Inn', said one. How wrong can you be? Premier Inns don't have views like that, visible – according to Irish construction-industry magazine *Build* – courtesy of a Dublin-based glassmaker.

> The new central London studio with its floor-to-ceiling windows offers an unrivalled view over the city skyline from Saint Paul's to the Gherkin and far beyond. SmartGlass International was called in to design and install a solar-control glazing system that would combat the negative effects of direct sunlight including glare and heat. SPD [suspended particle devices] SmartGlass offered the perfect solution and was installed in approximately 100 window panes. The glass façade can now be automatically dimmed from clear to dark controlling glare and solar heat gain while

protecting the studio inhabitants from the damaging effects of UV.

So, up yours, critics. Next?

'An odd mash-up of *GMTV*, *The One Show*, *That's Life* and *Newsnight*'; 'Bleakley's role is to laugh tinklingly at Chiles's jokes and express no opinions whatsoever'; 'Chiles even insisted on talking about the various clocks he could spot around the room, while Bleakley gazed at him, chemistry-ishly, with a dazzled grin. Although for a contract that size [said to be £10 million between the two of them], who can blame her?'

Some of those viewers who feel compelled to post their opinions on websites were no more complimentary, behind their *noms de plume*. 'Adrian might be the best thing to happen to television since chocolate laxatives'; 'You stretch, yawn, turn on the TV and see Adrian Chiles's face gurning back at you. Enough to put anyone of his breakfast'; 'Seeing the inane grin on the orange-painted face of Bleakley plus, if you left the sound on, a stream of drivel delivered in her accent – that would make anyone want to jump off a high building'.

Some halfwit using the name 'grincher' posted, 'He can't help it, he is half Croat,' in case anybody looking at the site, run by one of our 'quality' newspapers, wanted to know just how low it could go and still not be moderated.

Meanwhile, back at the ranch, the good folk in ITV PR were polishing their keyboards, although not entirely sure how to spell 'licence' when it's a noun.

ITV Breakfast is a wholly owned subsidiary of ITV plc and was formerly known as GMTV. ITV Breakfast holds the license for the Channel 3 breakfast day part. Transmitting daily from 0600–0925, our programmes are designed to reach our core housewife audience with a diverse range of programming strands.

On weekday mornings, our newly launched *Daybreak* show features a unique combination of news, showbiz, features, sport, celebrity interviews and live bands. At weekends, the focus moves to children, with the pre-school strand *The Fluffy Club* followed by *Toonattik* for older kids.

Breakfast is a key day part for advertisers, reaching consumers while they are at their most alert and most likely to act upon the messages that they receive.

Hands up all consumers who believe they are at their most alert and most likely to act on advertising at breakfast time. All right, hands up all who don't think that. Thank you.

All front-of-camera people on the show had been warned to avoid attempts at naff humour. Naffness is in the eye of the beholder, of course, as in this posting from Anmelia: '[We want a] bright pair on bright red sofa. Not a right pair in a plum role on a purple sofa, raisin (sorry couldn't resist it!) not a lot of interest.' Then we read, 'Perhaps they should concentrate Daybreak into a suppository perhaps.' And, even more enigmatically, 'Mind you they say you can't have FUNeral without FUN in it, well it is not making me smile.'

What was that about wanting to jump off a high building?

Adrian and Christine had more flung at them by these people: 'Muppets'; 'Sausage Face and Goofy'; 'god's gift, both wooden'; 'marmite couple'. On the other hand, the very delightful 'double-oh-heaven' wrote, 'Fabulous viewing. Consummate professionals. Morning has definitely broken, in the most delightful way.'

According to one reviewer, the pair seemed 'incredibly cosy' on their sofa, and 'touchy-feely', with St Paul's and the Gherkin in the background. Relaxed, at ease, looking as though they're enjoying themselves, comfortable in each other's company, elegant (Christine), sharp (Adrian) – these were terms used by those who don't have vitriol for breakfast.

As Adrian crossed the studio floor for the sports news, he said, 'This is more of a man's thing.' Christine's reply was, 'So I'll just sit here and file my nails, then. And this is the part where he walks and talks.'

At last, an alternative to the BBC. I love the BBC morning news but it can be dull. ITV was dreadful – cheap, cheerful, lacking the intelligence to make it work. Daybreak was very watchable. Christine and Adrian are very talented, witty, and intelligent.

So, not all posting persons do it to be horrid.

'I love it'; 'I think it's brilliant'; 'I thoroughly enjoyed it'. But, we have to admit, positives were outnumbered by negatives, on blogs, in papers, and in the new medium beloved of those who can't get enough of themselves, Twitter: 'I loved GMTV, hate Daybreak. Adrian Chiles needs eye test, he has to lean forward and makes it obvious that he is reading his script'; 'The set looks like London Tonight when I was 15. That's almost 15 years ago'; 'Well I can safely say ITV have lost me as a morning viewer — Daybreak is awful! I'm switching to Eamonn Holmes'; 'Would love to have seen the "Every crew member must laugh at Adrians quips" memo'.

That's one side of the twits (or tweets if you prefer). Here's the other: 'Daybreak was a bit raw. I'm going to give it time. Liked old faces but new ones need settling time'; 'Liked what I saw – fresh, & Christine & Adrian are just so good together'.

About one million viewers on average watched the first *Daybreak*. The *Guardian*, bless it, ran a poll: is *Daybreak* a great start to the day or a good reason to go back to bed? Whether or not *Guardian* readers are the best judges of popular TV, especially those who can find the time and energy to answer a poll on line, we cannot say, but the result was 77 per cent for going back to bed. The next poll after that result was 'Is it cool to wear clothes made of meat?'

By the Thursday, ratings were slightly down at 891,000 average (22 per cent) while the BBC equivalent was slightly up. *Daybreak* had had a Yorkshire terrier in the studio, and now moved on to an outside broadcast, recorded in the evening, with Prince Charles and Camilla at Clarence House. Christine asked HRH what he thought of climate-change doubters: 'I find it extraordinary. To me it seems sensible to take a precautionary approach. Clearly something is going very wrong. I would say to sceptics: "It may be convenient to believe all these greenhouse gases we are pouring into the atmosphere disappear through holes conveniently into space, but it doesn't work like that." '

Adrian, who had worn an open-necked shirt for Tony Blair, was in collar and tie for this one, but his interviewee proved just as adroit at avoiding the question. Adrian said, 'These are tough economic times and people are trying to save every penny. And they might say, well it's OK, you've got a huge garden and lots of money, it's easy for you to go green.'

The prince replied, 'You could say that. But then on the other hand all this week I've been looking at all these marvellous examples on the ground of very disadvantaged communities which have actually taken all this sort of thing in their stride.'

HRH then reinforced Adrian's point by showing off his vegetable patch. All organic vegetables, of course, and used by the royal chefs in the royal kitchen, but we were left to wonder how many royal gardeners had been involved in their production. HRH seemed bemused when Adrian told him he had no vegetables for his tea, and was there a courgette going. If not, he'd settle for that small onion over there, which would at least be a royal onion, and therefore very special.

As they were leaving, the prince did say that, quite seriously, Adrian was to help himself.

The commercial launch of *Daybreak* and *Lorraine* took place on Monday, 13 September.

Daybreak has been one of the most significant programme launches this year and Adrian Chiles and Christine Bleakley hosted the launch with Lorraine Kelly. The event showcased some of the new elements found in the ITV Breakfast slot which has had significant investment to drive more viewers to ITV1. Adrian & Christine were joined by some of the Special Correspondents including Sue Jameson, Political Editor, Lucy Verasamy, Weather & Environment Correspondent and Steve Hargrave, Entertainment Editor. In Something Cool Before the Kids go to School, guests were shown the new hottest gadget for Christmas; the AR Helicopter drone, a four rota helicopter controlled over wifi and the iPhone.

In its third week, an average total of 3.2 million viewers watched *Daybreak*, a 19.7 per cent audience share, the same as the previous week, but not as good as *GMTV* in the same week one year before. There was also a drop in the key viewing demographic of young mums.

'Audiences are definitely deserting it,' said one source, while an ITV spokesman said '*Daybreak* has made a strong start in a very competitive breakfast-television market, with viewing figures for its first three weeks up on the annual average for *GMTV* and positive feedback on the new show from our viewers.'

'It's too studio-based,' said another industry expert, but David Kermode, editor of *Five News*, commented, 'New things take time to settle. The show they have in three months' time will be very different from the one they have now. I was at *BBC Breakfast* for three years and it took a year to close the gap on *GMTV*.'

The business people were busy, selling sponsorship.

An excellent programming environment, coupled

with high indices among key audiences, makes
Daybreak & *Lorraine* the natural choice for
sponsors who want to reach adults, women,
working women, housewives, parents, families and
children. The frequency of exposure on *GMTV*
tends to be higher than that on other channels, with
most of the sponsored properties appearing more
than twice a day.

Slight typing error there. Shouldn't that be *Daybreak*, not
GMTV?

Minute TV is an innovative sponsorship opportunity
exclusive to ITV Breakfast. It is a one-minute
programme in the form of tips, advice and hints.
The sponsored items run for one week, and have
had excellent results in terms of awareness and sales
uplift for featured sponsors. Pre-recorded one-
minute 'break bumper'. Flexible creative presented
by well-known faces. Five-day sponsorship
available. Two 10-second credits per day. Book
Solus/first[-]in[-]break ads for maximum impact.
Online & mobile messaging opportunities.

And you thought television was all about *Dad's Army* and
The Antiques Roadshow. No, no. Come on. Move with
the times.

A dedicated in-house sales team enables us to
concentrate on the unique strengths of the ITV
Breakfast package. A close working relationship
with our editorial team means that we are in a

unique position to tie-in advertising with programming content. We know our product inside out and advise agencies on specific upcoming opportunities where their advertising can work in a distinctly relevant environment.

And still the bloggers tapped their keyboards, their fingernails dripping venom.

Get rid of them both or if we must have them teach them how to sit on a sofa and try to look intelligent, Adrian always looks as if he is having trouble reading the auto cue and is in danger of falling off the sofa, and she seems to have trouble keeping her skirt down. What a rubbish show.

I must say, I am at a complete loss as to why the presenters of Daybreak are always laughing so much. What on earth is so funny? Perhaps they're laughing at the mugs who paid them so much to front this quite frankly bizarre show. Or maybe there is a carbon monoxide leak or maybe they're just wired from the early starts. Give it a rest guys, I can't take much more of Christine's massive teeth!!! I am giving them 1 more week before I switch to BBC Breakfast for good.

Carbon monoxide? Perhaps he means nitrous oxide.

'Time to get rid of this awful programme and it's awful presenters. Seriously, do you know of ANYONE who actually likes this show?'; 'Oh my word you pro GMTV lot give it a rest! It's gone, over, done, watch something else & move on!'; 'Legends! the pair of them! Never understood the criticism these two get. They always seem to have a laugh and make jokes (some of them aint the best). Always seem to not care if they make fools of themselves.'

So, who likes *Daybreak*? According to Facebook, Jayne does, and she also likes social-networking computer games such as *FarmVille*, computer dating, romantic novels, *Emmerdale*, *Coronation Street*, *Dancing on Ice* and, in music, Peter Andre and 'anything really new and old'. Julie, another *Daybreak* fan, likes the same sort of games, also Ant and Dec. Dawn likes coriander, Joni Mitchell, Michael Bublé, Mary Poppins, *Come Dine with Me* and *River Cottage*. Oh, and *FarmVille*. Val likes Billy J Kramer, Cliff Richard, the Beatles, the Famous Five, *Strictly*, *Springwatch* and *Dragons' Den*, and lists Adrian Chiles as one of her activities, but not *FarmVille*. There must be a lifetime's work here for a university sociology department.

So, let us turn to an expert for his opinion.

Daybreak is crap. I am a media student and im pritty sure us guys who dont have a job in the buisness could have divised a 100 per cent better show than Daybreak even with the same presenters. It looks like a 6 year old made the set, a monkey is choosing content and all that space in the studio – they still sit next to each other. So I have a right to come on here and critisise the show because I know more than most of you about how Tv shows are put together.

What a shame that media students who know more than most of us about TV shows, yet don't have a TV job, also don't seem to know very much about spelling, grammar and punctuation. Oh, well, can't have everything.

Whatever spin might be put on the figures by ITV, there did seem to be a bit of reverse swing in the cloudy atmosphere. If numbers that looked down were actually up, or that looked bad were actually good, there was no doubting the fact that *Daybreak* had not performed as well as had been hoped. According to the *Daily Star*, one remedy was for Christine to 'sex it up' by sitting closer to Adrian on the sofa. Closer? She'd be on his knee if she got any closer. According to the bloke in the pub, having seen the two of them clowning around in one-piece padded suits like sleeping bags with legs, it was too like *The One Show*.

After watching Adrian, Christine and Lucy Verasamy take the new driving test, which Adrian passed (by doing some research beforehand) and the girls failed, another bloke in the pub agreed with that assessment. Talking dog, canine potting pool balls by running around the table, woman eating record number of chicken wings – funny, but is it breakfast television? And, by the way, what exactly is breakfast television?

By mid-October 2010, the vultures were hovering. Vultures don't have saliva and so cannot drool over a thirst-crazed zebra, but their media equivalents were dribbling enough to start a new river. Newspapers reported with glee the audience figures: average 700,000 viewers for *Daybreak*, while *BBC Breakfast* had 1.8 million and, at the eight o'clock peak, 2.6 million for the BBC compared with *Daybreak*'s 900,000.

That ol' ginger nut had to put his oar in. Apparently, he was deeply disappointed by ITV, Christine, Adrian, everybody, as he told some BBC people at a conference. 'I don't understand what they were thinking. What was there was fine. *GMTV*'s audience knew what they wanted. They're not highbrow, news-hungry viewers. They had an opening of a million viewers and it's gone down. You only get one chance to open a show and it has not worked.'

Would Christine still be on the sofa at Christmas? Adrian had his football, but what would Christine do if it all went wrong? Someone alleged to be a close friend said, 'She is ambitious. She thought leaving the BBC would make her more high-profile. But she knows she has to stick it out.' With close friends like that, who needs a PR agency?

One oft-touted new role for her was as host of *The X Factor*. Some papers reported that she was indeed being 'lined up to replace Dermot O'Leary'. Such a move would depend on whether Dermot accepted Simon Cowell's offer to host *X Factor USA*. This he was expected to do, bearing in mind that Lord Cowell of X was himself rumoured to be leaving the UK show to concentrate on the American version. Whatever happened at *Daybreak*, Christine could number Cowell and top boss Peter Fincham among the life members of her fan club.

Peter Preston in the *Observer* wrote that the answer was obvious:

But pause before pulling the curtains on *Daybreak* too fast. These are early days – and what's wrong is clear enough to put right pretty fast. The core

audience for the *GMTV/Daybreak* slot is mums
getting the kids off to school. In short, women
viewers. But Chiles sits there like the Sultan of
Solihull surrounded by beautiful women: Chrissie
two inches along the sofa; fragrant newsreaders,
reporters, weather forecasters – and leftover Kate
[Garroway] from *GMTV*. Eye candy quotient for
men: 10 out of 10. Sex appeal rating for
housebound mums: zero.

The official view from inside ITV was positive, as we
might have expected.

The ratings have settled and a solid launch has been
achieved. Currently, *Daybreak*'s audience is broadly
in line with *GMTV*'s audience, as we had
anticipated. Now begins the task of steadily
growing the ratings. Breakfast viewing habits are
notoriously difficult to change and this process will
take time, but we are convinced that our new
offering will win over the breakfast audience.

Down the years we have conducted a great deal
of research investigating the wants and needs of the
breakfast audience. This has all been channelled in
to the making of our new show.

We have also invested heavily in research that
demonstrates the unique benefits of advertising at
breakfast-time. Our research programmes have
proved that consumers are more likely to remember
ads if they have seen them at breakfast-time, and
perhaps more importantly, they are more likely to
act upon those messages. In recent years we have

ADRIAN CHILES AND CHRISTINE BLEAKLEY

turned to cutting edge neuroscience techniques in order to explain this phenomenon and have discovered that the brain is fundamentally more receptive to advertising messages at breakfast-time. In short, this research proves that consumers are more likely to remember, like and understand commercials if they see them early in the day.

So, we were wrong about how alert we thought we were in the mornings, and some of us can't understand half the commercials at any time.

Whatever the views from head office and the pundits, most people were noticing a change on the show. The two presenters seemed calmer, not so nervous. Sticking it out seemed a perfectly good option, especially as *BBC Breakfast* was planning to move up to Salford. With the greatest possible respect to Greater Manchester and all who sail in her, such a move would be bound to affect the quality of guests who were willing to appear on the show at that time of the morning. Most breakfast-TV guests are reasonably handy for London studios. *Daybreak* was certain to benefit.

ITV could hardly wait, but *BBC Breakfast* was in no rush. It would be kept in London for as long as possible, to put pressure on ITV. An ITV spokesperson said, 'ITV has made a long-term investment in new breakfast programming and, after over five years of decline for *GMTV*, *Daybreak* is already closing the gap in year-on-year decline after just one month, with housewives and children, male and younger audiences.

'We look forward to building on this start and welcoming new audiences to *Daybreak* and *Lorraine*.

ADRIAN CHILES AND CHRISTINE BLEAKLEY

'*Daybreak* has a first-class presenting team and any suggestion that it will be changing is completely untrue.'